I0192645

THE
BATTLEFIELD
OF THE MIND

The Battlefield of the Mind
By Pastor Mark Spitsbergen, ThD, MS
Copyright © 2026 by Abiding Place Ministries, San Diego, CA.

ISBN - 979-8-9944098-0-0

2nd Edition

Address correspondence to:
Mark Spitsbergen
Abiding Place Ministries
2155 N Campo Truck Trail, Campo CA 91906
www.AbidingPlace.org
AwakeSD@me.com

All rights reserved.
Interior and Cover Layout by Graham Creative
Cover by Jake Smith

THE
BATTLEFIELD
OF THE MIND

Pastor Mark Spitsbergen, Thd, MS

Table of Contents

Introduction

God has given us great spiritual freedom from the dominion of sin and the power of Satan. Through the new birth, we were translated from the kingdom of darkness to the Kingdom of Jesus Christ[1]. We are now empowered to stand up against all of the enemies of God and live the life that Jesus has purchased for us. Jesus bore our sins in His own body and completely destroyed Satan's claim over our lives. Satan may attempt to reclaim our lives like the Pharaoh of old, but God has become our defense and our Deliverer.

Jesus made the way for us to live the heavenly life and be continually filled with all that pertains to His life and godliness[2]. He has brought to us the glorious and eternal life of God through the power of the Spirit of Holiness. Religion attempts to downplay the radical and total deliverance that we have received by describing salvation in terms of men's personal experiences instead of the

[1] (Col. 1:13)
[2] (2 Pet. 1:3)

Word of God alone. However, experience is not a legitimate witness against the truth of God's Word. The experiences of men are convoluted by their unbelief and lack of consecration to the ways of God. They allow so many things contrary to the Word of God to have a place in their lives and then redefine salvation based on their experiences rather than defining their lives and experiences by the Word of God. Every promise and blessing of God is contingent on meeting the conditions attached to those promises and blessings.

God has called us to His Kingdom and to His holiness and given us both the divine wisdom and power to live our lives in Him. There is a life that we can learn to live in Christ Jesus. The life of Christ Jesus and the ability to live His life is given to us by the power of the Holy Spirit. The very ways of God expressed in our lives are referred to as the fruits of the Spirit. The fruits of the Spirit are the ways of God that He desired mankind to have from the beginning. For we are His creation, created in Christ Jesus for good works that God prepared beforehand so that we should walk in them.

"In other words, God has prepared the works that believers will do, and Christ has prepared believers to do them."

(C. Campbell, 2012).

There is a warfare that we must engage in. Jesus showed us how when He was tempted by the Devil in the wilderness. We engage and win by the Word of God and by the Spirit of God. All that is in the world – the lust of the flesh, the lust of the eye, and the pride of life – wages war against the work of God that has been accomplished in our lives. Fleshly lust from the prince and the power of the air wars against our souls, but God has shown us how to engage and win every time. Just as Adam and Eve, in their pure and innocent state, were assailed by temptation, so the born-again believer must endure the fleshly lusts that war against our souls. Although we have completely escaped the rule of sin and death, Satan is still the prince and the power of the air. He is the god of this world who works in the children of disobedience, and he desires to gain back dominion over the saints' lives as well. In the midst of this great conflict, the Holy Spirit, our Teacher and Leader, teaches us perfect obedience to the Word of God. If we are going to live the life that has been given to us in Christ Jesus, then we must be willing to receive all that God has supplied to us. It all begins in believing that "He who the Son sets free is truly free." He has made us more than conquerors. He has given us the ability to overcome all evil just as He overcame.

The miracle of being an overcomer and overcoming just as Jesus overcame is found in believing God's Word. We must be willing to believe that we have truly been "washed with the waters of regeneration and renewed in the Holy Spirit." We must be willing to believe that the everlasting blood of the New Covenant is far greater than any power of the demonic realm of sin. There is no freedom for the person who believes and confesses that they are still bound to the slavery of sin. Through such a confession, Satan and his sin and death are given dominion, and the Word of God and reign of Christ Jesus are denied. There is no freedom for those who refuse to embrace the whole counsel of God. The lies that Satan teaches bring all who listen into bondage to His ways – it's only the truth of God's Word that sets free[3]. The miracle of salvation only becomes a reality because we are willing to agree with the Word of God that brings the miraculous results of faith.

The first man, Adam, was shaped from the dust of the Earth by God in order to bring forth the human race. God gave Adam dominion over all things in the Earth and a special place of ruling alongside Himself over His creation[4]. It would be from one man and his wife, Eve, that God would bring forth the whole of the human race. God would have one big family in humanity who would all be related to one another physically and spiritually. The beauty and splendor of God's purity and glory was reproduced in Adam – He was created with God's inward

---

[3] (Jn. 8:32)
[4] (Ps. 8:4-8; Gen. 1:26, 28)

likeness (צֶלֶם, 'selem') and outward appearance (דְּמוּת, 'demut'). However, Adam lost the inward likeness of God when He disobeyed. As a result, he and Eve died spiritually. Everything about the ways of God were corrupted in their lives, and the world came under the dominion of Satan. Every holy and pure thing that God created after His likeness became twisted by satanic power. All that He had made holy and pure was perverted within the nature of man. Still, God, in His great love and mercy, promised to restore man to the glory and purity of the inward likeness that he had before he rebelled against God's ways. He promised to redeem man and recreate him in His inward likeness. He would give mankind a new heart and a new spirit and write His laws in their hearts and minds. God would do this by the miracle of a new creation. He promised to wash away the sin and destroy the power of death and the rule of a twisted nature that possessed mankind. He would make, as it were, a new race of men through His only begotten Son, Jesus. Through the miracle of redemption, the blood of Christ Jesus would deliver and set free all those who would believe from every claim of sin and death.

Although we have been completely set free from the power of Satan, we still have the memory of sin. We also must learn how to properly deal with the knowledge of good and evil, which was forbidden by God, who desired man to only know good. In a place where there was only good, evil was to have no place. However, the right of choice was there. There was the opportunity to choose to obey and live or to choose disobedience and die. Satan and his demonic forces set their trap of temptation, and Adam fell for it. Every person faces the issues presented by the knowledge of good and evil every day. The only way to properly deal with it is through complete submission to the Holy Spirit. There was a choice that God gave Adam: the Tree of Life or the Tree of the Knowledge of Good and Evil. In many respects, we deal with the same choice every day. We choose whether we will do things God's way and obey Him, or go our own way that leads to destruction. Many have never truly set the battleline between good and evil and continually fall prey to the snare of the wicked one. Many who have been born again simply do not know what side they are on.

Redemption brought us back to the place where we are spiritually united with God. Disobedience and evil took men into the realm of spiritual death, but through the blood of Jesus, the life of God has been restored to us. Where we were once dead in our trespasses and sins, God has made us alive again to His ways of life. His nature and ways have been reborn in our inward parts. Our inner man which was once dead in sin and iniquity has been raised up together with Him with His inward likeness. We have been born of His Spirit and now live by the life of God. We have been begotten of His Word, which conveys to us God's own thoughts, desires, and will. He has given us a new heart after His own heart so that the wellspring of our lives might be filled with His thoughts. God has written His laws upon our hearts and minds so that we might hear and do His Word and continually be flooded with those things that are according to what He thinks. God has made our bodies His tabernacles where He now dwells. God has made our inner being the place that the rivers of His Spirit and glory pour forth unto the world.

We now have the choice: we can now believe what God has said and embrace a new and divine life in which we are one with God. The alternative is to continue with a religious mindset that has little regard for the change that is ours and rather chooses to confess some dimension of bondage to sin and death. If we want to walk with God and please God, then we must fully embrace what He has spoken. Without faith it is impossible to please God, and this kind of faith begins with agreeing with God. It is this faith that empowered Enoch to walk with God. It is this same faith that brought to pass the inward resurrection in our lives and raised us up together with Christ Jesus. If we will agree with Him, we will have a new kind of confession about who we are as a new creation. We will believe and confess that He has put His thoughts in our minds and in our hearts so that His thoughts have become our thoughts and His ways our ways.

One of the most fundamental spiritual rules is that if

we walk in the counsel of the ungodly, their deeds will ultimately establish themselves in us and we will stand in the way of sinners. Praise God that there is forgiveness of sins through the blood of Jesus Christ. However, if we persist in the sin we will surely find our habitation not in God but in the place where the wicked dwell – those who scorn man and God[5]. Every thought that is contrary to the ways of our God, the counsel of men and demons, must be recognized as foreign and cast down as treason against God's kingdom. Each person must make a clear distinction between what is of God and what is of the demonic realm. The Spirit of the Lord is still saying: choose this day whom you will serve.

---

[5] (Ps. 1:1-2)

His Laws Are Written Upon Our Hearts and Minds

God has put His thoughts in our minds, and in our hearts He has established them. How? Through the new birth. When we were born again, He wrote them on the tablets of our heart and mind, which is our inner spiritual being. The prophets of old spoke of the day that a New Covenant would come – a day when men would be turned back to know God and would serve Him with all of their hearts. On that day, God would make men His own dwelling place and give them a new heart and a new spirit. That day has come! God has put His thoughts in our minds, so that we should no longer walk in the vanity of our minds, being alienated from the life of God[6]. We have been born of the Holy Spirit to have the mind of God. We have been given the mind of Christ and the mind of the Holy Spirit. The spiritual mind has been given to us so

---

[6] (Eph. 2:3; 4:17; Col. 1:21)

that we may freely know all that God has given to us[7]. He has written His laws on the tablets of our hearts. Now God's peace, which is the manifest effect of the rulership of the Holy Spirit, is to be yielded to so that He may rule our hearts and minds. We have been born of the Word of God and His Word is to have first place in our thoughts. We have not only been begotten again by God's Word, which is the expression of His thoughts, but His Word dwells richly in our hearts[8]. Through this New Covenant, He has put His nature in our inner being and He has written them upon our minds and hearts[9]. They are not written on tablets of stone, as in the Old Covenant, but on fleshly tables of the heart – this is the New Covenant purchased by the blood of Jesus![10]

Who can be so bold as to say they have the mind of God? Who can proclaim that they know the thoughts of God, and are submitted to them? Are not these things concerning the knowledge of God far from us and completely out of reach? For the Scripture says,

"Oh the depth of the riches both of the wisdom and knowledge of God! How unsearchable are His judgments, and His ways past finding out! Who has known the mind of the Lord?"   *(Romans 11:33-34)*

---

[7] (Rom. 8:5-7; 1 Cor. 2:12)
[8] (Col. 3:16)
[9] (Heb. 8:10; 10:16; Eph. 4:24)
[10] (2 Cor. 3:3)

Yet we can confidently say that those who have been born of the Spirit have been given this mind of Christ and have been renewed in the knowledge of the Lord![11]

> *"We have put on the new man, which is RENEWED in KNOWLEDGE according to the image of Him who created Him."*   *(Colossians 3:10)*

Now, in Christ Jesus, we can boldly say that we have "all the treasures of wisdom and knowledge"[12]. These treasures of the knowledge of God have all been hidden in Christ Jesus, and only those who have Christ dwelling in them have been given this knowledge that belongs exclusively to God and has been revealed to us by His Spirit. Flesh and blood cannot boast of this knowledge. This knowledge is not found within our intellect or in the realm of our own reasoning. This knowledge cannot be discovered through human endeavors – this is the knowledge that belongs to God. It is this knowledge that brings the revelation of His thoughts:

> *"For My thoughts are not your thoughts, neither are your ways My ways," says the Lord. "For as the heavens are higher than the Earth, so are My ways higher than your ways, and My thoughts higher than your thoughts."*   *(Isaiah. 55:8-9)*

[11] (1 Cor. 2:16)
[12] (Col. 2:2-3)

Yet now, through the New Covenant, God has put His Holy Spirit in us, who brings to us all that the Father has. The Holy Spirit shows us what eyes have not seen and ears have not heard, nor have the hearts of men understood – but now He has revealed them to us by His Holy Spirit[13]. This knowledge of God came to us as a gift through the indwelling of Christ Jesus. We have been joined unto the Lord and made one with Him, and through the Spirit, we now have the knowledge of the Lord: the knowledge of who He is and the knowledge of His ways. By the working of the Holy Spirit, we grow in this knowledge in all wisdom and spiritual understanding. We have been given an understanding heart that we might know Him! And now, if we will put on the Lord Jesus Christ, the revelation of "all that the Father has" will be revealed to us by the Holy Spirit![14]

Through the free gift of salvation, we have been given entrance into the unsearchable depths of God's wisdom and knowledge. All those things in God that men could never discover or attain are now revealed to us by the Holy Spirit. "For the Spirit searches all things, yes, the deep things of God" and He reveals them to us[15]. The Holy Spirit has come to reveal everything that belongs to the Lord Jesus and our heavenly Father to us[16]. Many will say

---

[13] (1 Cor. 2:9-12)
[14] (Jn. 16:15; Gal. 3:27; Rom. 13:14)
[15] (1 Cor. 2:10-11)
[16] (Jn. 16:13-15)

that this cannot be. They will look at the arm of flesh and say, "Impossible!" Others will strain and wrestle to achieve these things, but they will remain out of reach until we accept on bended knee what God has freely given. Then, in obedience to the Word, we confess those things that God has spoken, and faith arises and makes the impossible possible. This knowledge that is too wonderful for us arises and says within our hearts, "Christ is in me!" In this communion of faith with the most high God, we discover the unsearchable riches of Christ!

Even as the heavens are higher than the Earth, the knowledge of God far surpasses man. Men can give themselves to study and develop their intellect to the highest level of academic achievement, but they will not begin to even touch the realm of God's knowledge. Human intellect can never enter into the realm of divine intellect. Even the foolishness of God is greater than the wisdom of men, but there is a realm of the Spirit that has been given. If we will yield ourselves like little children, then we will be taught of God. If we forsake the realm of self-reliance and no longer lean on our own understanding in an attempt to find our own answers, then we can walk in the divine intellect, the mind of God. We have been trained to logically and rationally figure out and solve the problems set before us, but this is not the way of God. We must forsake our way and our thoughts if we are going to be found in Him having His ways and His thoughts. We must learn to depend upon the Word of God and the Spirit of God for our answers and direction. We can trust that God is going to lead us and guide us. Many of our decisions are already made for us by what God has commanded us to do in the Scriptures. Many of our questions are answered for us in the Bible. **However, we must also learn to take everything to God in prayer and wait upon Him for direction concerning those things that God has not already made known in His word.**

We must learn to yield to God and be led by the Spirit of the Lord, and not by our own ideas. If we are going to walk in the things of the Spirit, then we cannot be guided by things that belong to mere human intellect. The natural mind of men can never be subject to the mind of the Spirit because they are foolish to the natural mind[17]. The Spirit of the Lord will show us things that go far beyond the boundaries of our natural understanding. The Spirit of the Lord will show us the answers that the Father has for all our problems, questions, and concerns. He will lead us in His wisdom and knowledge and will give us divine understanding. He will reveal the highest heights and the deepest depths of the knowledge of the Lord. Oh the depths of the riches and the wisdom of the knowledge of God that has been put into our hearts by the Holy Spirit – how unsearchable they are to the human intellect! The condition to function in the mind of Christ is that we

---

[17] (1 Cor. 2:14)

surrender ourselves to the guidance of the Father, to the word he gave us in the Bible. It is the Holy Spirit alone who can teach us and cause us to know and understand all that God has done for us when He established His ways within us. He does this through the instructions found in the Word of God. If we attempt to know the Mind of God through our own efforts and reliance on our own knowledge we will distort and pollute what God has spoken. Instead, we must come and sit at His feet and learn from Him.

It is a great challenge for a person to stop being reactive and not operate out of their own impulses. The realm of self-defense and quick-thinking will not work here. We have been given this great privilege to understand "with all of the saints what is the breadth, and length, and depth, and height; to know the love of Christ that passes all knowledge, and be filled with the fulness of God"[18]. It is more than just a submission to the Holy Spirit during an altar call or a declaration of surrender to God. This kind of knowledge that comes from knowing the love of Christ demands a surrender to being one with Christ Jesus, a oneness that came as the gift of salvation[19]. When we give ourselves over to the love of Christ, we have a trust in God that compels us to wait on God and be led by Him. If we remain in a posture of humility before God

---

[18] (Eph. 3:18-20)
[19] (Jn. 6:56; 17:21-23; 1 Jn. 3:24)

and look for His direction, we will have it. There in the stillness of this submission, we hear the thoughts of God rise up from our hearts by the Holy Spirit. The Holy Spirit brings into our remembrance those things that Christ Jesus has spoken, and He speaks directly to whatever situation we find ourselves in. The knowledge of God and the mind of Christ will not be hidden from us if we come to expect that God will direct us and speak to us. Our posture before the Lord and consecration unto Him must always be to look for His leadership and guidance.

All of the depths of God's knowledge and His fullness is found in the love of Christ; not just His love for us, but His love in us. We are to know this love, not in part, but in every dimension of His eternal glory and power[20]. We are not to possess only some of the knowledge of Christ, but we can be filled with all the knowledge of His will that is found in the love of Christ. This knowledge of God is ours through the mighty working of His power within us – and all we must do is yield. We can learn to rely upon the unseen world of the Spirit. We can see what is unseen by the faith of God that has been given to us. With confidence and assurance, we can freely receive all that the Holy Spirit desires to reveal[21]. All these things can only be received as a free gift – otherwise, they are unavailable and out of reach! They cannot be earned. They are received,

[20] (Eph. 3:17-18; 1 Cor. 13; Jn. 13:34; 1 Jn 3:14, 16)
[21] (Jn. 1:16; 14:26; 16:13-15; 1 Cor. 2:10-16)

because we believe that they are ours – given to us liberally by the Spirit.

God has supplied us with the Holy Spirit in an unlimited way: like rivers. It is in this context that God has given to us all of His blessings and promises. It is in learning to give ourselves to this flow of the Spirit that we mature in all that has been divinely supplied. Taking on the identity of Christ and the heavenly life gives us an expectation and confidence to receive what only God can give. We are not of this world and we have to be willing to be consecrated to living a heavenly spiritual life. The wisdom and revelation that the Holy Spirit gives causes us to see the inheritance that He has in us[22]. Being obedient to the heavenly vision and calling will result in all that God has promised. That we are in Christ and He is in us should be a conscious reality that we live in. Recognizing that He is present in our lives brings an expectation that all that He can do will be done for us. If we are going to have His thoughts, then we must dismiss our thoughts and hold tightly to His Word. This is the act of obedience that the Father is looking for. This is submission to do the will of the Father and a willingness to be taught by the Holy Spirit.

---

[22] (Eph. 1:18)

The Heart: The Wellspring of Our Thoughts

As the natural heart is central to our physical life, so too is the spiritual heart central to our spiritual life. The Bible describes two different conditions of the heart: there is a hard stony heart (also referred to as an uncircumcised heart), and there is a soft heart of flesh (circumcised heart). Jesus described the spiritual condition of the hard stony heart as the source of everything that defiles a person. The stony heart is the heart of those still under the dominion of sin and death. From the unredeemed heart proceed the evil thoughts of adulteries, fornications, murders, thefts, covetousness, wickedness, deceit, lasciviousness, an evil eye, blasphemy, pride, and foolishness[23]. This is the condition of every unredeemed person. Until you are born again, the heart remains bound by sin and death. It was from this stony heart that the continual wicked imaginations of the thoughts of men so

---

[23] (Mk. 7:21–22)

grieved God that He destroyed them from the face of the Earth, sparing only Noah and his family[24]. God described the heart of man as being wicked from his youth[25] – all of which was a testimony of the evil nature that ruled the heart of mankind. The wickedness of man's heart was described by the prophet Jeremiah when he said,

> *"The heart is deceitful above all and desperately wicked – who can know it?"* (Jeremiah 17:9)

The only hope for a cure was the promise of the coming redemption in which God would restore men to union with Himself. The prophet Jeremiah described the change of the heart through the redemption that was yet to come when he said, "I will put My Law in their inward parts, and write it in their hearts, and will be their God, and they shall be My people"[26].

Paul likened the heart of man to the tablets of stone on which God wrote His commandments. Instead of God's Law being written on tablets of stone, they were written on fleshly tablets of the heart. The fleshly tablets of the heart came into existence when we were born again. It is in this new heart that the Word of faith is placed so that we may believe with the heart and confess with our

---

[24] (Gen. 6:5)
[25] (Gen. 8:21)
[26] (Jer. 31:33; Heb. 10:16)

mouth[27]. Whatever is in the heart will be spoken by the mouth. More than the Word of God just being recalled from memory, or "hidden in our heart" it is written in our hearts so that we might not sin against God. This became a living reality when we were born again and His Word was written on our hearts[28]. This all took place when we were born of the incorruptible Seed by the Word of God[29]. His Word now dwelling in us by His Spirit, works with His divine power in all who will believe[30].

It is with the heart that we believe or doubt, but because we have believed, the Word of faith is in our heart and mouth. Whatever is in our heart is what we think. Whatever is in the heart is what we speak. When we were born again, Christ Jesus came to dwell in our hearts[31]. Now that He dwells in our heart, His Word dwells there also[32]. Therefore our meditations are set upon God's meditations and our thoughts are to be governed by the words of His mouth.

The heart is the hidden man or the inward spiritual being of our lives[33]. When we were born again, Paul likened the change that took place in our heart as a circumcision of the heart, which removed the body of the

---

[27] (Rom. 10:6-10)
[28] (Jn. 3:3; 1 Pet. 1:23; Jam. 1:18; Jer. 31:33; Heb. 10:16)
[29] (1 Pet. 1:23)
[30] (1 Thess 2:13)
[31] (Eph. 3:17)
[32] (Col. 3:16)
[33] (1 Pet. 3:4; Jer. 31:33)

sins of the flesh[34]. The wicked and deceitful heart that is alienated from the ways of God was completely cut away by the circumcision of Christ. The heart was purified when we obeyed the truth of salvation[35]. Now we are truly able to ascend unto the hill of the Lord, because we have a pure heart, purified by the new birth[36]. God has taken away the stony uncircumcised heart and given us the new heart of flesh, because He gave us a new spirit and placed His Spirit within us[37]. We now serve God with a pure heart. We love with the love of God out of a pure heart[38]. We call on God out of a pure heart[39]. We know and are able to understand God because He has given us a pure heart[40].

So then where do the wicked thoughts come from that the redeemed have to deal with? They come from without! They come from the demonic realm – all that is in the world[41]. The realm of darkness no longer rules us from within, but it attempts to influence us and dominate our lives from without. All that is in the world where the spirit of disobedience now reigns would attempt to gain dominance over our minds by plaguing our thoughts with their wicked imaginations. But God has given us the

---

[34] (Col. 2:11; Rom. 2:29)
[35] (Ac. 15:9; 1 Pet. 1:22)
[36] (Ps. 24:3-4; 1 Pet. 1:22-23)
[37] (Ezek. 36:26)
[38] (1 Tim. 1:5)
[39] (2 Tim. 2:22)
[40] (Mt. 5:8)
[41] (1 Jn 2:16; Titus 2:12)

power to deal with every wicked imagination and high thing that would attempt to exalt itself against the knowledge of God and the obedience of Christ Jesus. Instead of yielding ourselves to the mind of the demonic world, we instead yield ourselves to the mind of Christ. Each time we are faced with the choice, we have the wisdom that comes by the word as our defence. We have the shield of faith and the sword of the Spirit to stop every deception of our enemy. The truth of God's word that sets free is our battle axe in every confrontation. We have allowed the good Seed of God's Word to be received into our heart, and it brings forth the great increase and harvest of God's life and goodness in every situation[42].

We must keep our hearts with all diligence, because it is from our hearts that the issues of God's life springs forth. God has made our hearts as a fountain of sweet water from which His words of life and Spirit pour forth. Jesus described the gift of God and the work of salvation as a wellspring[43]. God placed His very life, which is eternal life, in our inward being. He described it as a continual flow coming forth from our lives. It is His life, His word, and His Spirit that come out of our innermost being. It comes forth from our bellies, or the inner womb, of our existence as rivers of living water[44]. The very vital force of our lives – both our spirit and our heart – are united

[42] (Mt. 13:23)
[43] (Jn. 4:14)
[44] (Jn. 7:38-39; cr. Ac. 2:33)

together with the Spirit of the Lord[45].

---

[45] (1 Cor. 6:17; Jn. 17:21-23; Eph. 4:4)

The Challenge

What God has done must be accepted as true and then believed and put into practice. The first step of putting something into practice is speaking or declaring it. The confession: "I am saved," is one of the first steps of putting into practice the gift of salvation[46]. The confession: "I am in Christ" is our agreement with God's Word that will result in the faith that puts it into practice. There are too many people that continually backslide in their minds. They begin with a good confession and then enter into various stages of doubt and unbelief. They find themselves continually influenced by the opinion of others, religion, or even demons. Men say that the promises and blessings of God are out of our reach. Satan lies against the truth, continually slandering the Most High and His saints. We have to determine that we are not what others say we are, but what God says we are. We must believe that we are what God has described us to be in His Word. It should be

[46] (Rom. 10:9-10)

God's thoughts, given to us by His Word, that rule what we think and say.

God has freely given us all these great things that pertain to His glory and character in Christ Jesus. Greek phrases like ἐν χριστῷ ("in Christ") and ἐν χριστῷ Ἰησοῦ ("in Christ Jesus") are found 86 times in the New Testament and when the pronoun is used in place of Christ, such as ἐν αὐτῷ ("in Him"), we find the expression many more times. The strongest possible emphasis is placed on our union with Christ Jesus, but we must be willing to believe! The faith of the New Covenant is finding our whole existence in Jesus. It is "in Christ" that God has proposed that we live our lives and define our existence! If we will, then we will discover the miracle of the life of Christ Jesus living in us and through us.

If we remain in a state of trying to earn what God has given – or equally, believing that it will only come to pass when we die and go to Heaven – then it will never be ours. Both confessions are wrong and are contrary to the miracle of faith. We must embrace what Jesus purchased for us and believe that it is all ours now – yes, all of His fullness![47] It is not earned or deserved, nor is it waiting for us sometime in the future – His great salvation is ours now! It is just as wrong to place salvation and union with Christ somewhere in the future as it is to seek it by the works of the Law. Too many confess the work of grace that

---

[47] (Jn. 1:16; Col. 2:10)

has brought salvation but describe it as "now but not yet," and still place themselves under the dominion of sin. They may claim a positional standing with God, but they reject the experience that is now a living reality dwelling in us by His Spirit who He has given us. They will accept that all that He has done has been imputed, but they will refuse to accept that He has imparted His life into us now.

Those things described by the prophet Ezekiel became a reality by the miracle of salvation in our lives because we believed the Word of God, and the Holy Spirit worked the miracle. The simplicity of faith believes that we have a new heart and a new spirit simply because God says we do. The old is gone, and the new has come. The fallen state of the heart and spirit that we inherited because of Adam's sin has been removed. God has restored to us a new heart and a new spirit after His own inward likeness[48]. We believe it's true because God has said it is, and He has the power to make such a miracle happen. It is in the simplicity of faith that comes by the Word of God that the Holy Spirit creates the miracle that God has promised – the miracle that God decreed when He said,

> *"A new heart will I give you and a new spirit will I put within you. I will take away the stony heart out of your flesh, and I will give you a heart of flesh. And I will put my Spirit within you and cause you to walk*

[48] (Eph. 4:24; Col. 3:10; 1 Jn. 3:24; Col. 1:27; 2 Cor. 5:17 etc)

in My statutes and you shall keep My judgments and do them." (*Ezekiel 36:26*)

This is what God has done for all who will accept the salvation that is in Christ Jesus: it is the same for all, both Jew and Gentile. It is the inward resurrection and the new life in Christ Jesus[49]. God took the sinful heart away and gave us a new heart, but we must believe it and confess that this is what God has done. For it is with the mouth that confession is made unto salvation[50]. We cannot backslide in our thinking based on all the reports of men! We do not put our faith in a future work of grace, but one that we have been given now. We know and believe that today is the day of salvation, not "someday in the future." This good news must be our confession and our song of thanksgiving every day.

The uncircumcised heart of stone that belongs to those who are unredeemed cannot know the ways of God nor be submitted to them. The stony heart cannot be sensitive or yielded to the Spirit of God. The stony heart of the unregenerated natural man cannot receive the things that God has freely given to us in the new creation. If we are imprisoned with the words of men and demons and live in doubt of what God says, we will never live in the miracle of faith. If we are willing to believe that we have

---

[49] (Col. 3:1-3; 2:12)
[50] (Rom. 10:10)

something less than the new heart of the new covenant, then we will not receive those things that have been freely given. Rather, we will live our lives locked away in the prison of Christian religion and unbelief. We will live our lives dominated by the words of men and demons rather than the Word of God. It is time to stand up and boldly proclaim all these words of life. If God said it, then it's true. Stop waiting for another day – that day has come – all you must do is believe! Will Satan lie against the truth? Will his attacks and his meaningless words of defeat assail our thinking? Yes, but what we must do is hold fast to the confession of our faith and not let it slip, no matter what kind of evidence or slander Satan may throw at us. We must be willing to rise up with the weapons of our warfare, which are mighty in God. With the shield of faith and the sword of God's Word, nothing can defeat us.

Jesus has come and removed every part of the stony heart – it does not exist today! The circumcision of Christ has removed the sin and separation we once had and has made us one with the Lord[51]. Therefore, harden not your hearts that have been made new, and hear His voice today! Step into your inheritance – do not allow yourself to be turned back by the giants that are in the land or by the fear of men. There is no rebellion within you that would refuse the voice of God if you have been born again. Instead, your heart is united with the heart of God. There is only

---

[51] (Col. 2:13)

yieldedness and tenderness in your heart toward the voice of your Beloved. This must be your disposition – let no one take your confidence! We are not from beneath – we are from above! We are not of this world – we are citizens of Heaven. This is the faith wherein we stand. It is with this faith that we can comprehend and lay hold of all the promises of God. We have been transformed from an old man into a new creation. It is this new man that has the mind of Christ and is yielded to the Holy Spirit. We no longer live – it's the life of Christ Jesus that we now possess. The voice of unbelief that would question what God says must be refused. Satan is still questioning God and His motives, just as He did with Adam and Eve at the first. It is time to let the Word of God be your confidence and trust. We must not listen to the voice of the deceiver. Just as Jesus threw down every assault and temptation of the Devil with the Word of God, so shall we[52]. All we must do is be willing to believe that what God has said is absolutely true and the faith and miracle of faith will work within you[53].

You are born of the Word and the Word is written on the tablets of your heart. The words that are the expressions of the Father's heart must be allowed to rule your heart and mind. The word of Christ must be your governor. If you have to fight all of the lies against the

---

[52] (Mt. 4:1-11)
[53] (1 Thess. 2:13)

truth that are assailing you all day, then fight. God's truth and power will triumph over all those lies of men and demons! The Word of God will overthrow the lies and the darkness will not be able to remain in the light of His Word. Having done all to stand: stand, and don't back down – you are more than able to overcome and possess this land of grace. You have been given the strength of the Lord and the power of His might. The same Word that framed the universe dwells in you right now – speak it. The eternal Word that was incarnated into flesh dwells there in your heart right now and He has overcome!

God's thoughts that are conveyed to us by His Word must become our meditation and be that which we believe about ourselves. It is a wonderful privilege to know what God is thinking and to be certain of what He wants us to do. It is God's Word that conveys all these things to us. Those things that came out of His heart and have proceeded forth from His mouth have been grafted into our souls. That Word, which is quick and powerful, would instruct every dimension of our passions and attitudes if we will yield to its training. The living power of His Word that is Spirit and life would now master all our thinking[54]. We must let His Word work with its divine power by believing what He has said[55]. The Word is near us at all times – in our hearts and in our mouths. Therefore, we

---

[54] (Jn. 6:63)
[55] (1 Thess. 2:13)

31

must refrain from speaking other things that are lies against the truth. Jesus overcame because He chose to live by the Word. Living by the Word must be our choice too. It is this Word of truth that is in our hearts and mouths – these words are His thoughts that are higher than our thoughts. Therefore let us forsake all other thoughts and have His alone. Let God train you in His knowledge by agreeing with His Word at every point. Let the understanding of Almighty God be your understanding now.

Jeremiah spoke of this day that would come when God would build His temple in the heart of men. God would no longer tabernacle in a tent that was made with hands, but would come and live and dwell on the inside of man. Jeremiah said, "I will put My Law in their inward parts and write it in their hearts…"[56]. Our inner being – the nature and construction of who we now are in Christ – has been hard-wired with the ways of God. The Law of God is not merely some rules and ordinances that God came up with so that men can get along and do what is right. The laws of God are the expressed ways of the nature of God and the divine code of life that He designed. These laws that express His nature could never be written with ink and be obeyed – the heart of man had to be changed. The wellspring of the thoughts had to be supplied with a new kind of fountain: the fountain of

---

[56] (Jer. 31:33)

God's life. Therefore, God wrote His ways and established His thoughts in our hearts and minds by imparting His nature, which is His Spirit. He inscribed His nature – not on tablets of stone, but on fleshly tablets of the heart. These things cannot be understood, much less truly observed, if they are written merely on tablets of stone – they must be written within the heart and nature of men[57]. The unseen realm of the nature of our life, which is the source of all our motivations and inspirations, has been recreated in righteousness and true holiness. However, faith that produces the miracle will never be activated until we believe and say that it is so. If we are going to walk in the ways of God, then we must believe that we have been miraculously changed by the power of God and begin to give ourselves to the conduct that God has described in His Word. If we are willing to obey God, then we will find that the Holy Spirit is a real Companion and Teacher who will lead us and guide us into all the ways of God. The Holy Spirit will train the new man in all the ways of God so that we might grow up into all the fullness of Christ Jesus.

---

[57] (2 Cor. 3:3)

The Battlefield of the Mind

As those alive from the dead and born of the Spirit of
God all that now exists within us is our own will, Christ
Jesus, the Spirit of God and the love of the Father. Yet, all
that is in the world – the lust of the flesh, the lust of the
eye, and the pride of life – are opposed to the Spirit of
God[58]. The Holy Spirit is the opposite of the spirit that
rules the unregenerated heart. In the bondage of the
unregenerate heart and spirit, a person cannot do what
they will to do because they are ruled by a fallen nature[59].
When we are born of the Holy Spirit, we must be under
His rule and not walk after our own ability – otherwise,
we will surely fail. Thus we are in the midst of warfare, and
the battlefield is a battle fought within our thoughts. If we
walk in the Spirit, then we will not fulfill that which is
contrary to the Holy Spirit[60]. The question is: whom will
we obey? We must gird up our thoughts and be ready to

[58] (1 Jn. 2:16)
[59] (Gal. 5:16)
[60] (Gal. 5:16-18)

stand against three areas that will assault our thought-life and attempt to lead us away into captivity:

1. The direct assault of Satan that comes at us as fiery darts. Even Jesus was tempted by Satan, but it was the word of truth that broke the power of the satanic lie and cast down the lies and unholy thoughts that questioned God.

2. The hearts of wicked unredeemed men are also a source of every vile thing and wicked imagination[61]. These things of men pour out in a modern society like a flood from every walk of life.

3. Finally, there are the memories of the past that can plague and assail the redeemed with tormenting thoughts of grief, of accusation and temptation. Satan, the rebel against God, would continually proclaim to the listening ear that he still has power over our lives. He is the accuser of the brethren and the slanderer against God and His people.

God has made it possible for us to be strong in His strength, so that we may effectively deal with these unholy thoughts and find ourselves more than conquerors in every battle of the mind[62]. Fleshly lusts will war against our souls that have been purified, but the Lord has given

---

[61] (Mt. 15:19)
[62] (Eph. 6:10; 2 Cor. 10:4)

us His own strength and power to effectively deal with all the powers of darkness and keep ourselves unspotted from the world[63]. When evil thoughts or any form of temptation arise, we are empowered to put it to death, because it is not part of who we are[64].

Our thought-life is of vital importance to us and to God. It is within our thoughts that the seeds of our deeds are planted. What we meditate on will ultimately take shape in our deeds. Our thoughts lead the way into what will be the conduct of our lives. It is first in our thoughts that we must deal with the counsel of the ungodly. It is here that we will encounter the lies and deceptions of Satan and of men. The temptations that would come to pollute our purified souls begin as thoughts, whether they are audible suggestions or unheard imaginations. These diabolical deceptions that would try to infiltrate our pure minds must be cast down. It is here in our thoughts that the battles are won or lost. Therefore, it is essential for us to define for ourselves what things we are going to think on, and what things we are going to cast down. If we are not careful, the strongholds of the unredeemed life could take us back under their dominion, and we would lose the place of communion and fellowship with God[65]. God, who is perfecting everything that concerns us, will teach us to hate evil and love righteousness. The One who upholds us

---

[63] (Eph. 6:10-12; 1 Pet. 2:11; 2 Cor. 7:1; 1 Jn. 3:3; Jam. 1:27; 1 Jn. 5:18)
[64] (Rom. 8:13; Col. 3:5; Gal. 5:24)
[65] (Heb. 8:10; 10:16; 2 Cor. 3:3; 6:16)

will keep us from falling and will cause us to triumph over every evil thing. He will teach us every good way and every good path. We will learn to walk in the mindset of the Spirit and think of that which belongs to the life of God[66].

Our thought-life should be a sacred realm of conversation with the Lord. We should think about those things that pertain to His life and godliness and be taught by God. The meditations of our heart should be holy and acceptable to our Lord[67]. We should think about these things: what is true, honest, righteous and pure – all that God has spoken[68]. We should meditate upon His Word day and night that we might prosper in the ways of God and be successful in everything that He has purposed for our lives[69]. Every thought that would grieve the Holy Spirit should also grieve us, and be viewed as an imagination contrary to God and the new heart. Through the power of the Holy Spirit, we have been given divine power to bring into captivity everything contrary to the obedience of Christ and the spoken Word of God. However, if we hold on to things like unforgiveness or some lustful thought and do not cast it down, it will take dominion over our thoughts. Out of unforgiveness, for example, every imagination that is a violation against

---

[66] (Rom. 8:5-7; Php. 4:8)
[67] (Ps. 19:14)
[68] (Php. 4:8)
[69] (Jos. 1:8-9; Ps. 1:2; Isa. 59:21; 51:6-7; Rom. 10:8; Deut. 30:14)

relationship will continue to work and affect our conduct, unless its power is broken through repentance. We will never be overtaken by these evil things if we will allow the love of Christ and His peace to rule our hearts and minds. When the love of Christ Jesus rules we will not allow these things contrary to His love to steal our peace. That which grieves the Holy Spirit will also grieve us and we will not allow it to continue to work within our minds, but instead we will cast it down.

God gives us godly counsel that will overthrow every ungodly thing that would attempt to rule us. He tells us to walk in His love and mercy, which impacts every area of our lives. For example, the area of relationships can be the most challenging part of our lives. Yet, if we simply walk in the love of God that is supplied by the Holy Spirit, every challenge can be met with forgiveness. We only have to be willing to say "yes" to God and forgive one another, even as He has forgiven us. All we must do is agree with Him, and forgiveness and mercy will flow effortlessly from the soul of anyone whose mind is submitted to the Word and yielded to the Holy Spirit. God will strengthen us to love and forgive at every turn of reproach and violation. Similarly, we have to deal with every area of sin and that which opposes the ways of God. However, if we regard lust and covetousness as anything other than an offense to God, and give them place within our thoughts, then these wicked devices will force themselves upon us and go unchecked by the power of God that resides within us. Our will stands between victory or defeat! If we will the will of God, we will always defeat everything that opposes God's will for our lives. We have not been given this mighty power of God to mitigate what Satan would attempt to do through his treachery and deceit, but to demolish it! Once again, if we walk in the love of God, it has no abusive and ungodly lust in it, but it fulfills all that Father has willed.

Satan will throw his darts of wickedness and deceit, and we must have a shield of faith to quench all his fiery thoughts[70]. Satan wages a war against the saints to pollute and taint our thoughts with his unholy deeds[71]. He speaks out threats and slanders against God and His saints. He is the spirit that works in the children of disobedience, and his fabricated lies must be identified and cast down. We must recognize that these are not our thoughts, but the thoughts of the wicked one. They must be renounced and sent away by the blood of Jesus or they will lead us into acts of defiance against our God and King and allow Satan to reconstruct his stronghold. Satan will attack us with these thoughts – either by a direct assault, or indirectly through the unredeemed – but God will always cause us to triumph over them.

One of the indirect ways that Satan attacks us is

---

[70] (Eph. 6:16)
[71] (1 Pet. 2:11; Eph. 6:11; 2 Cor. 11:3)

through the unredeemed, whose hearts are wicked, and who are a direct link to the spirit of disobedience. Out of the heart of the unredeemed proceeds every evil thought and imagination[72]. We must be careful not to be influenced by the lusts and the wicked imaginations of the lost. It is our responsibility to not only refuse the counsel of the ungodly but also all their influences. We must recognize the importance of not walking in their counsel or being influenced by their worldly lusts or wicked imaginations. This is truly what it means to not be of the world. The world must be crucified to us. We must recognize that spiritually we have come out from among them and are separated unto God. We can have no fellowship with the unfruitful works of darkness, but instead we should reprove them[73]. Although the lost are the target of God's affection – and we are sent by Him to reach them – we must take the word of our testimony and the blood of the Lamb, or their influence could turn our hearts instead of the power of the Gospel turning them.

Another source of unholy thoughts is the memory of our past sins. Although all our sins are washed away, our memory can bring them back into our minds. Satan can both condemn and entice us through those memories, and we must be ready to deal with these things the moment that they come. When these thoughts arise from

---

[72] (Eph. 2:2; Mt. 15:19; Mk. 7:21)
[73] (Eph. 5:11)

past experiences, repent of the deeds that were done as though you are repenting for the first time. Command the thought and the memory of sin to leave in Jesus' name. Let the Word of God wash your mind, and in the fear of the Lord these things will lose all their influence. It is in the fear of the Lord that we hold fast to the wisdom of God and the knowledge of the holy. If we submit ourselves to God and resist the Devil, he will flee from us!

We must draw the battleline clearly and certainly. We must always remain confident that our thoughts are aligned with God and all other thoughts are foreign. Thoughts of wickedness do not come from within our hearts but from outside – they come from all that is in the world[74]. Just as the thoughts of wickedness were used to tempt Jesus, these thoughts that come from the demonic realm do not belong to us or to our true desires. Our thoughts that come forth from our hearts are those things that are taught to us by God, and all other thoughts must be renounced and sent away. God both speaks to and through the new heart that He has given to us, and we cannot allow a mixture. The new heart is the place where God dwells, and His thoughts and deeds are in us as a wellspring[75]. Our hearts are God's dwelling place, the sacred room of His holiness; and out of it flow His rich treasures of life. We now serve God with a pure heart, and

---

[74] (1 Jn. 2:16)
[75] (Prov. 4:23; Jn. 4:14)

41

through it we know Him and fellowship with Him[76]. Out of this purified heart, we love the brothers with a pure love – and in Christ Jesus our relationships are untainted by deceit or vile imaginations from the demonic realm[77]. It is out of the heart that the issues of life flow, the wellsprings of the Spirit. We must guard our hearts like the temple guards of old.

At the core of all God's desires and commands for us is His desire that we would do everything out of love, and thus fulfill all His commands. It is "love, out of a pure heart," a love that He has given us by the Spirit of Holiness[78]. We must not let our hearts be polluted by unforgiveness or any other unholy thing. It is from the heart that we do those things that please Him, and so we must keep our hearts with all diligence. It is from the heart that we must forgive[79]. It is from the heart that we follow "righteousness, faith, love, peace, with those who call on the Lord out of a pure heart"[80]. It is from our hearts that our affections arise; and so all your affections must be for God – anything else is from beneath. It is with a pure heart that we see God[81]. It is out of a pure heart that we call on God[82]. It is with a true heart that we draw near

---

[76] (Mt. 5:8; Ezek. 36:26; Deut. 30:6; Col. 2:11)
[77] (1 Pet. 1:22; Heb. 10:22)
[78] (1 Tim. 1:5; Rom. 5:5, 7-8)
[79] (Mt. 18:35)
[80] (2 Tim. 2:22)
[81] (Mt. 5:8)
[82] (2 Tim. 2:22)

unto God[83]. It is from our heart that we believe[84]. It is from our heart that we forgive, and it is from our pure heart that we love one another fervently[85]. With a single eye of affection, let your whole body be filled with light. When darkness would come to attempt to lure your desires away, recognize the deception and the ploy of your enemy. Do not be enticed, but keep yourself in the love of God and the love for Him, obeying His commandments. These matters of the heart are of utmost importance to God, and we must be consecrated to keeping our hearts with all diligence, for out of them proceed the issues of life.

---

[83] (Heb. 10:22)
[84] (Rom. 10:10)
[85] (Mt. 18:35; 1 Pet. 1:22)

The Wisdom of God

From the Word of the Lord comes wisdom, and it is the Holy Spirit who will lead us into all the knowledge of God. There is nothing more valuable than wisdom – it is the first and most important thing in life[86]. It was by wisdom that God created everything in the universe, and it is by His wisdom that everything functions[87]. Wisdom is knowing what God knows and doing what He does. God calls out to us and asks us to receive the wisdom that He has: the wisdom that comes from the words of His mouth. Wisdom allows us to see the hidden things and understand the ways of His eternal life. He also asks us to look to Him and ask for wisdom in everything that we do, and promises to give it to us liberally if we ask in faith[88]. Wisdom will show us how to be successful in everything that God desires for our lives. Wisdom will give us sound judgment and allow us to see the goodness of God. We

---

[86] (Prov. 4:7)
[87] (Ps. 104:24; 136:5)
[88] (Jam. 1:5)

will know and understand the ugly consequences of sin, and the ways of death will be a disdain to us. Wisdom will allow those who have it to see things as they really are instead of how we might imagine them to be through human influences and satanic deception.

Wisdom gives us the ability to understand what things look like in the spiritual realm. It gives us a special ability to view life from God's perspective and to know the consequence of every evil thing. The wisdom that comes from above came upon the seventy appointed to help Moses and instruct Israel in the ways of God[89]. The wisdom of God allowed them to know the mind of God and to speak on His behalf. Wisdom that allows us to more perfectly visualize heavenly things was given to Bezalel so that he could make things that had never before been seen on Earth or experienced by men[90]. Paul prayed for this wisdom and spiritual revelation to be seen in our lives as well.[91]

Wisdom is one of the chief expressions of the Spirit of God dwelling in the lives of the men of God[92]. The Spirit of wisdom and revelation will give us the ability to see things and understand things that otherwise we could not grasp, because they are in the unseen realm of God[93].

---

[89] (Num. 11:16)
[90] (Ex. 31:3, 6)
[91] (Eph 2:15-21)
[92] (Ex. 35:31)
[93] (Eph. 1:18; Gen. 41:38; Dan. 4:8; 5:12)

When Moses laid his hands on Joshua and imparted the anointing that he had received, Joshua was filled with the spirit of wisdom[94]. With this insight and understanding, he discovered the word of God's own authority in His mouth and the sun and moon obeyed him. The wisdom that God delights in is ours today if we will lay hold on the ways of wisdom, which are the ways of God taught to us by the Word of God.

Wisdom can be called the secrets of God[95]. It is these secrets that He whispers to the hearts of His children. This wisdom cannot be found apart from a relationship with God, for it belongs only to Him and to those who seek after it[96]. The wisdom of God will cause us to turn from every evil way[97]. When we speak the Word of God and declare the ways of righteousness, we are speaking the wisdom of God[98]. When we meditate on God's Word, we are giving our thoughts to the wisdom of His own thoughts[99]. God desires that we take hold of truth and for it to be the makeup of our soul; and then, when truth is established in the inward parts, He causes us to know wisdom[100]. God established His truth in our hearts when the Spirit of Truth came to reside within us. Christ Jesus,

---

[94] (Deut. 34:9)
[95] (Job 15:8)
[96] (Job 28:12-24; 38:36; Prov. 2:6-7)
[97] (Job 28:28; Prov. 3:21-23)
[98] (Ps. 37:30)
[99] (Ps. 49:3)
[100] (Ps. 51:6)

who is the truth, now dwells in us, and God has made Him to be our wisdom[101]. Men cannot know wisdom unless they know the fear of the Lord[102]. He cannot receive the instruction of wisdom until the Word of God becomes a delight to his soul[103]. He must love righteousness and hate iniquity – otherwise the wisdom of God will be a dark hallway that he will not venture down. God has given us all this ability when we were created anew in Christ Jesus, but we must be willing to follow on to know the Lord to grow and develop in it.

God greatly desires for all of us to receive wisdom. There could be no greater gift for us to receive than to be ruled by the wisdom of God. God's wisdom so desires to fill our lives that it lifts its voice and cries out to the sons of men to allow it to come in[104]. Wisdom, like the Spirit of God, is a wellspring of life to those who have it[105]. If we are going to walk in the wisdom of God, then we must submit ourselves to the humility of God and recognize that the thoughts and insights of the human intellect will not lead us into the wisdom of God[106]. Wisdom will not dwell with a person who scorns or despises their neighbor[107]. There is no envy, strife, or self-importance in

---

[101] (1 Cor. 1:30)
[102] (Ps. 111:10; Prov. 1:7; 9:10)
[103] (Prov. 2:1-5)
[104] (Prov. 8:1)
[105] (Prov. 16:22; 18:4; Jn. 4:14)
[106] (Prov. 11:2; 23:4)
[107] (Prov. 11:12; 14:6)

this wisdom that comes down from above – for it is pure, gentle, and merciful; teaching peace and the ways of God[108]. God will correct us and teach us to walk in all of His ways. If we will not despise the chastening of our God, we will respond obediently to the instruction that He gives. It is in this relationship with God that we learn to walk in the direction and the insights of the Lord instead of foolishly pursuing our own way[109]. Just as the Holy Spirit cries out, wisdom cries out to us, pleading with us to walk in God's instruction. In the love of God and knowledge of who He is, we will not ignorantly ignore what God has freely and abundantly given to us.

If you take hold of the wisdom of God and live by every word that proceeds from the mouth of God, the Holy Spirit will be your Keeper and Guide. He will lead us into all the glorious and eternal ways of that which God knows[110]. We may freely eat from the fruit of His lips and enjoy all the good fruits of His wisdom and insight. Only those born of the Spirit can partake of His wisdom and knowledge. The person who sits in darkness is alienated from the life and knowledge of the Lord. But when God made this New Covenant through the last Adam, Christ Jesus, He poured His life and wisdom into our hearts. He has given us liberally of all His fullness, but we must yield to the Spirit of the Lord. Men in ancient times sought

---

[108] (Jam. 3:15-17)
[109] (Prov. 3:11-13; 29:15; Heb. 12:5; 1 Cor. 11:32)
[110] (Prov. 2:5)

diligently for – and could not obtain – this wisdom that is now a gift within our hearts. They sought for it as one who looked for treasures of silver and gold; should we take for granted these unsearchable riches of the Lord? Once we discover the riches of wisdom, then those things that have come from the thoughts and meditation of the Lord will be our daily delight[111]. Once again, this wisdom is not found in the world of men and has nothing to do with the intellect of men – rather, this is the divine intellect of God. This wisdom and knowledge is poured into our hearts by the Spirit of the Lord[112]. The knowledge of the Most High that has been given unto us allows us to understand a far deeper dimension of life than what the mortal eye can see or the heart of men can comprehend: we understand righteousness, judgment, and equity; yes, every good path[113]. When we were created in righteousness and true knowledge after His image through the new birth, this wonderful gift entered into our hearts[114]. Now we know and understand how to walk in all the paths of righteousness and how to dwell in true holiness by the Spirit of the Lord. The seven-fold anointing of the Holy Ghost has filled our hearts with a wellspring of a quick understanding in the knowledge of the Lord[115].

---

[111] (Prov. 2:6; 8:30)
[112] (Prov. 2:10)
[113] (Prov. 2:9)
[114] (Eph. 4:24; Col. 3:10)
[115] (Isa. 11:2-3)

The Knowledge of Good and Evil

The Bible introduces the knowledge of good and evil in a paradoxical way. It is set in the context of that which is forbidden to man, yet at the same time is something that belongs to God. For man to receive it in the first place would be an act of disobedience. This act of disobedience would be the means by which Satan would gain dominion over all humanity. The consequence of disobedience was spiritual death. While Satan claimed that the knowledge of good and evil was the means by which man would gain wisdom, instead the spiritual death and the knowledge of good and evil opened their eyes to their nakedness and they entered into fear, and shame. Instead of gaining wisdom, they had rejected it. The knowledge of good and evil is difficult to separate from the spiritual death that took over Adam and Eve. However, we know that God has the knowledge of both good and evil, and in His knowledge He loves the good and hates the evil. Man, dead in their trespasses and sins through disobedience, came to love the evil and hate the good. Like Adam, their spiritual condition causes them to run and hide from God. They refuse to come to the light, because their deeds are evil and they have altogether refused that which is good. When we are born again, the dominion of sin and death is destroyed, but the knowledge of good and evil remains. Now by the Holy Spirit and the wisdom that He gives us, we learn to hate evil like God hates evil.

The issues of the knowledge of good and evil are highlighted each time we are confronted with the choice to choose the good and refuse the evil. We live our lives in the throes of dividing between good and evil, between light and darkness, obedience and disobedience, or righteousness and sin. It is the subject second in importance only to being redeemed and made a new creation. Now that we are restored in the inward likeness of God, every man still has a choice to make between good and evil. It seems that many doctrinal ideas suppose that once this life is over that such a knowledge and a choice will no longer be with us, but the Scripture does not support this idea.

Jesus showed us the life of consecration and submission to God that is essential if we are going to walk with God and do what is pleasing in His sight. The evil must be refused, and the good must become the way of our life in Him. God teaches us to hate evil and to love righteousness, but we must be willing to learn. Unless we will embrace the life of Christ and walk in the Spirit, this discernment will not be ours, and we will find ourselves continually caving into the demonic lies that suggest that sin is good. Men put evil for good and hate the light because they love evil[116]. God has brought us out of sin and darkness and filled us with His Spirit so that we may learn to choose the good and refuse the evil. God alone knows how to properly deal with the knowledge of good and evil. The Author of life understands the threat that evil is to all of life. That which appears to be good and desirable in sin will only work death and destruction. As for the unredeemed, even when they would do good, evil is present with them and the good that they would do is absent from them[117].

The paradise that God created for man to dwell in was filled with only good things, but when sin entered into the world, death also came with it; the two are inseparable. Sin will turn every beautiful and lovely thing into a world of destruction. God has invited us back into the paradise of relationship and union with Him, and now in this heavenly paradise of union, we must learn how evil sin is and refuse it. God, who also has the knowledge of good and evil, has given to us His knowledge, His wisdom, and His understanding so that we can deal with the knowledge

---

[116] (Jn. 3:19)
[117] (Rom 7:19)

of good and evil in the proper way[118]. The way to properly deal with the knowledge of good and evil is by the Holy Spirit who trains us to hate the evil and love the good; to refuse the evil and hold fast to the good. He gives us the wisdom to see the destruction of evil and its ultimate ruin and death. God has given us the choice. Set before us is life and good, and death and evil[119]. God has renewed us in His knowledge and filled us with His Spirit so that we would have a divine resolve to choose what God has chosen, to choose life and the good and walk in His eternal ways.

The knowledge of God is the knowledge of good, and it is clearly contrasted with the knowledge of evil throughout the Scripture. The knowledge of God comes to us by the wisdom of God, which is taught to us by the Word of God. We can only find the knowledge of God through the great redemption that has been given by the Living Word, Christ Jesus. He made the knowledge of God pleasant to our souls and brought to pass all of the wisdom described in the Proverbs. However, as the days of apostasy come upon us, men have less discernment between good and evil than ever before. They call that which is good evil and those things that are evil they call good. They also put darkness for light and light for darkness. This can be observed in every walk of life: in

---

[118] (Gen. 3:22)
[119] (Deut. 30:15)

government, the education system, and every social media. What is worse now more than ever is that this lack of discernment appears in the pulpits of our churches. Everywhere we look the knowledge of evil dominates, with no true discernment of the ways of God, who alone is good. Many would make the message of salvation something different from the liberation from sin and death. They fail to realize that it is the divine empowerment to fulfill the call of God to walk in obedience and truth. Even walking in the Spirit is not understood in the context of learning the ways of God. The Scriptures reveal that the knowledge of the Lord will increasingly be forsaken until they will kill the righteous and say that they do God a service. Those who preach the way of righteousness, which are the ways of God, are viewed as a hindrance to church growth and a reproach to the grace of God. Even as in the days of ancient Israel, but in a more subtle way, men regard iniquity and forsake the good. God's people are found loving evil more than good and lying rather than speaking righteousness[120].

Those who have been born of God and who walk in the Spirit of the Lord must depart from evil and do good[121]. We must learn to choose the good and refuse the evil[122]. We have been given the special diet of the good Word of God and the laws of the Spirit of Life have been

[120] (Ps. 52:3)
[121] (Ps. 34:14,27; 1 Pet. 3:10-11)
[122] (Ps. 11:7; 33:5; Isa. 7:15; Heb. 1:9; 1 Tim. 6:11; 1 Jn. 3:10; Prov. 15:9)

established within our hearts so that we may learn His ways. We have the unstoppable power of God dwelling in us so that we may overcome everything that belongs to the realm of darkness. The knowledge of God is ours, and it is only by His knowledge that the knowledge of good and evil may be properly dealt with. The deception of evil and the illusive lure of sin will lose all of its power as we are taught of the Lord and walk with Him. If we choose the way of God, the fruits of His knowledge will be revealed in our lives. The fruits of the Spirit and the fruits of righteousness will reveal that we are His trees: the planting of the Lord[123]. The day is fast-approaching that God will destroy everything that is evil and the Earth will be filled with the knowledge of the Lord as water covers the sea. Choose the knowledge of God, discern the destruction of evil, and come let us follow on to know the Lord.

---

[123] (Is. 61:30; Mt. 3:10; 7:17-19; Lk. 6:43; Prov. 11:30)

The Mind of Self

Jesus revealed His consecration to, and relationship with, the Father when He said,

"I can of My own self do nothing. As I hear, I judge, and My judgment is just, because I seek not My own will but the will of the Father who sent Me."

(John 5:30)

The realm of the self is one of the most misunderstood subjects and is often confused with the sinful nature and the flesh. However, the self is the essence of who we are as an individual, and it must be denied so that we may, as the servants of God, do His will instead[124]. God's ways are better than our ways, so we must forsake our ways to learn His. Unlike the flesh nature that was crucified with Christ, the self that makes us distinct from all other individuals goes on living forever. While we are here in our earthly

---

[124] (1 Pet. 4:2; Jn. 1:13; Col. 1:9)

sojourn, it must be denied so that we might perfectly yield to what the Father desires to teach us.

All of us have many choices that we can make about our lives and vocations, the things that we are going to do with our spare time, and how we are going to spend our money. By definition, none of these choices may have anything to do with a sinful action, but neither would they necessarily be the will of God for our lives. If we are going to follow Jesus the way that He has called us to follow Him, then our own ideas and choices must come to an end. We have to be willing to learn a servitude and a submission to God where we do it all His way. We must be willing to come to a place where we are not going to decide anything for ourselves again. If we are going to live out the life described in the Bible of being those who are the witnesses of the resurrection, then we must learn that we can do nothing of ourselves[125]. It is important that each of us understand how this impacts us individually with respect to the choices that we make and how we live our lives. We can make the whole subject simple by saying, "Walk in the Spirit and mind the things of the Spirit." However, the identification of those things that would exclude the Holy Spirit can be overlooked. We are either going to walk in the wisdom of God or we will walk in our own wisdom. We will either walk in the knowledge that God has or we will walk in our own knowledge. We will

---

[125] (Jn. 15:5)

either walk after the direction of the Holy Spirit or we will walk in our own direction. If we are willing, the Lord will show us how we can walk out His will for our lives in every area of life. He will show us how to turn our jobs into a mission field. How to glorify Him in our recreation time and in every choice and decision of life.

There was nothing evil about Jesus – no matter how He was examined, everything was perfect. Yet, even He denied Himself. Though He was one with God and God incarnate, yet He showed us the perfect submission of a Son who would live only by the will and direction of the Father. He would choose no earthly goal for His life other than to do the Father's will. How much more must we deny ourselves? We have spent our lives imitating men, and now we must choose to imitate God[126]. The mind and will of the self, which is not necessarily evil, must be submitted to the will of the Father. God the Father has chosen the best things for us, and we must do as He says if we are going to inherit them. As we have already said many times, we do not have the ability to deal with all of the opposition set against us; we must have the mind of God and the strength of the Holy Spirit. To have these far-superior things in our lives, we cannot make our own decisions or be led by our own instincts.

The most important thing about denying ourselves and walking in the mind of God is to believe what God has

---

[126] (Eph. 5:1)

said about us. All of our lives we have been receiving an identity from man. From the cradle to the grave everyone has their opinion about who we are and what we have the capacity to do. It is from all of these reports and interactions in society that we are given an identity of ourselves. Basically everything that we know about ourselves has been imposed upon us by the world that we live in. Now, if we are going to receive the identity that God has given to us then all of these things that we believe that we know about ourselves must be denied. We must be willing to embrace all that God has said about who we are and what we can now do in Christ Jesus.

When it comes to doing heavenly things and the things of the Spirit, we of ourselves can do nothing. Within ourselves, we function out of a natural intellect that is trained by life's experiences and circumstances. There is nothing wrong with a logical and rational mind, other than that it is severely handicapped and grossly limited when we want to consider the things that belong to the spiritual. With a natural mind, we can never properly deal with the craft of Satan who lies in wait to deceive us. Even more, the rational and logical mind will never understand the realms of faith – faith that walks with God and commands the wind and the waves such that they obey. Such a notion is foolishness to natural thinking[127].

Natural thinking determines what we can do on the

---

[127] (1 Cor 2:13-14)

basis of what we believe we have the ability to do within ourselves. The spiritual thinking that is given to us by the Word of God and the Spirit of God believes that we can do all that God has spoken. One of many examples is the Faith that says, "God will supply all that we have need of according to His riches in glory." Faith will call forth the provision of God and find it in the mouth of a fish[128]. To walk in this kind of faith, we must be taught of God. We must be willing to learn how to step beyond that which is limited to a natural realm. God wants to move us past the elements of the earthly into the dimensions of the heavenly, but we have to be willing to deny ourselves and step beyond the limitation of what we can physically and mentally do for ourselves and learn how to rely on the Holy Spirit. God will teach us to believe His Word and we will learn to step out and walk on the water by His direction.

That which is earthly and belongs to the realms of "self" is not necessarily bad; it is just limited and temporal[129]. God calls us to a radical life of trusting Him so we can learn to walk in the realms of the spiritual. We must deny ourselves to hear the Holy Spirit instruct us in those things that belong to the spiritual life. The way that men think is not the way that God thinks. The natural mind is governed by what it sees, hears, and has physical

---

[128] (Mt 17:27)
[129] (Rom. 15:27; 1 Cor. 9:11; 15:44)

60

evidence for, and therefore would not be submitted to the Spirit of God. We have to be willing to stop trembling with fear as we tightly hold on to our own ability and rather plunge into the vast expanse of the spiritual and walk in the Spirit. To do this, the self must be denied. The Bible does not describe the self as being put to death – it just needs to be refused so that we might learn how to function in a whole new way of life: the life of God[130]. The spiritual mind that accepts the impossibilities of the Word of God without the need of any other proofs far exceeds the limitation of what self can understand. The spiritual mind functions in a realm of faith and depends upon the unseen power of God to do all that God has commanded. In fact, faith does not work within the confines of a natural mind; faith is spiritual.

If we confine our thinking to those things that belong only to our own self-interest and self-preservation, then we will focus on those things that we can accomplish through our own efforts and abilities. These limitations of self-realization will then govern what we will believe and ultimately what we will do. Without being aware of it, we will even filter God's Word through the perspective of these self-serving interests. In this state, doubt and fear will govern us rather than the faith that comes by God's Word. Many of God's children are stuck in this place that has robbed them of their maturity in God. It has limited

---

[130] (Mt 16:24; Mk 8:34; Lk 9:23)

their confidence in God and dependence upon the Holy Spirit. It is impossible for the realm of self to live in a confidence in God that takes no thought for what they shall eat or what they shall wear[131]. It is a place of fear, condemnation, limitation, failure, and even defeat. There is little, if any, room for faith and submission to the Holy Spirit in the realm of carnal human thinking — where men seek their own interest and rely upon human abilities to accomplish their own goals. The natural mind is that state in which men hold on tightly to themselves to preserve their own well-being, and whose securities are their earthly possessions. The carnal mind and ways of men will altogether shut down those things that the Holy Spirit has come to teach us[132].

Anything that is taught to us by God concerning Himself is spiritual and in stark contrast to those things that we learn of men. All that the Holy Spirit does and ministers is that which is spiritual and eternal. One day, we will exchange a natural body for a spiritual body, but right now we must exchange a natural mind for a spiritual one. The things of the spiritual are foolishness to the natural mind, because they are not governed by natural laws. Everything concerning the will of the Father is spiritually discerned. The spiritual is the unlimited realm of divine ability and supernatural provision in which

---

[131] (Mt 6:25,31,34)
[132] (1 Cor. 3:1-2)

nothing is impossible[133]. We are commanded to learn this new way of thinking, but we must recognize those thoughts that would confine us to the limitations of what we can do of ourselves, classify them as doubt and unbelief, and deny them[134]. God is a Spirit, and we must interact with Him in the realm of the spiritual. Any interaction with the Holy Spirit or manifestation of the Holy Spirit is by definition spiritual. Knowing that we are to walk in the Spirit and be led by the Spirit is evidence enough that God demands us to be spiritual in the way that we think and conduct ourselves. It is the Holy Spirit who teaches us the spiritual and gives us access to the realms of the spiritual: from which all the gifts of the Spirit flow. We learn to think according to the spiritual (or, the manner in which God thinks) by the Word of God and the guidance of the Holy Spirit. The spiritual mind is the mind of the Holy Spirit, the mind of Christ, the life governed by the Spirit of God – where every thought is brought into captivity to the obedience of Christ and the will of the Father.

---

[133] (1 Cor. 2:13-15; Mt. 19:26; Mk. 9:23)
[134] (Eph. 1:3; 1 Cor. 2:14; 14:1, 12)

Renewing of the Mind

When we consider that the redeemed have the mind of Christ, what is Paul referring to when he speaks of the renewing of the mind? There are two places in the Epistles of Paul where he instructs us to be renewed in our minds[135]. The instruction is given to those who are born of God. Knowing that we are holy and acceptable to God, we should not be conformed in any way to the world. In fact, we should be transfigured by the renewing of our minds. Paul is most certainly speaking of a new way of thinking. The Greek word μεταμορφόω ('metamorphoo') is the result of the renewing of the mind, it's a transfiguration: "...and be transfigured ('metamorphoo') by the renewing of your mind"[136]. Jesus was not transformed on the mount – rather, He was transfigured[137]. (To be transformed μετασχηματίζω (metascheatizo)) is to be changed from one thing into

---

[135] (Rom. 12:2; Eph. 4:23)
[136] (Rom. 12:2)
[137] (Mt. 17:2)

another. This word is used four times in this context in the New Testament[138]. Jesus' interaction with the Father while He was praying defines transfiguration. So instead of being conformed to the world by agreeing with its thinking and actions, we are to be transfigured by interaction with God[139]. Paul is referring to an entirely new way of thinking, especially about ourselves and our relationship to the world. Similarly, as a "new man" recreated in righteousness and true holiness, the same message is underscored. The former lifestyle should not be part of our lives anymore. Instead of living and thinking after the "old man," the unregenerate state, we should think according to the "new man," who is recreated in the image of God. This is a new kind of thinking that comes from interacting with God as a new creation.

It is always best to attempt to understand the meaning of words not just from their context, but also from the original language from which it was derived. Paul testifies that we have been made new and that we are renewed many times. He used the same word that is found in Romans 12:2, "renew" (ἀνακαίνωσις, 'anakainosis'), several times. The Greek word ἀνακαίνωσις ('anakainosis') is found in Titus 3:5. Similarly, ἀνακαινόω ('anakainoo') is used, which is derived from the same root: καινός ('kainos'), found in 2 Corinthians 4:16 and

---

[138] (2 Cor 11:13,14,15; Phil 3:21)
[139] (Rom. 12:2; 2 Cor. 3:18)

Colossians 3:10. Paul testifies that through the washing of regeneration we were "renewed" (ἀνακαίνωσις, 'anakainosis') in the Holy Spirit[140]. This speaks of an event that took place from which we have benefited from a brand new life in Christ Jesus. The same is also communicated to us in Colossians 3:10 in which Paul says that we have put on the "new" because we have been "renewed" (ἀνακαινόω, 'anakainoo') in the knowledge of God – specifically in the knowledge that we have been created after the image of God. Also, just as the inward man that has been raised up with Christ Jesus is "renewed" day-by-day, so also then is the mind that is part of the inward being that was changed when we were born again. Therefore just as our inward man is renewed day-by-day in our relationship and interaction with God, even so our minds are renewed. The message of being "renewed" is in light of having already been made new, as in a new creation.

Finally, a similar Greek word, ἀνανεόω ('ananeoo') is used by Paul in Ephesians 4:23. As a result of being made a "new man" (καινὸν ἄνθρωπον, 'kainon anthropon'), we are to be renewed in the "spirit of our mind." Now that we are born-again, we must renounce and cast down those things belonging to the former lifestyle – the vanity (verse 17) and the darkness and blindness (verses 18-19) – and instead learn the obedience of Christ Jesus. The message

---

[140] (Tt. 3:5)

of Ephesians 4 focuses on our growth and maturity in Christ Jesus (verses 12-13). This is also in light of being strengthened by the Holy Spirit in our inner being and coming into the fulness of God[141]. This is all relationship language, the result of interacting with God. It is the work of the Holy Spirit. In fact, we are being renewed by the Holy Spirit in our minds as He stirs us and empowers us to think differently about ourselves. The Holy Spirit teaches us to refuse all of the influences of our former life. The former lifestyle is contrary to the new person that we are in Christ Jesus, and it must be put off and resisted in every way. We are supposed to think in a new and different way after the mind of the Spirit.

When we think of our mind, we immediately relate it to the way that we think. How we think about ourselves and God is very important to God and is essential to our growth and development in God. Our lives are sacred to God. We are the temples of the Holy Ghost and we must recognize how important our thoughts are to God. The way that we think has a profound effect on our communion with God and our faith in Him. It is time that we start thinking on a higher dimension and not on earthly things[142]. Our minds must be consecrated to the life that God has given. We cannot be conformed to this world and meditate on those things contrary to the ways

---

[141] (Eph. 3:16, 19)
[142] (Col. 3:1-3)

of God. We must instead be transfigured by the renewing of our minds[143]. We have been renewed in the knowledge of God, and we need to think accordingly[144]. We have been renewed in the Holy Ghost, and in Him we are renewed in the spirit of our mind so that we can think according to those things that God has made us to be in Christ Jesus![145] Just as we wait upon the Lord and our strength is renewed, our minds are renewed by putting on the new man through our daily interaction with the Holy Spirit[146]. Like our inner being that is renewed day-by-day as we mature in the things of the Holy Ghost, so our thoughts and the way that we allow ourselves to think is also renewed[147]. The living Word that has been inscribed in our hearts and in our minds must be allowed to rule the way that we think.

Consecration to the ways of God is essential to the renewing of the mind. The renewing of the mind is all about the way that we think and the way that we perceive ourselves and the world around us. It is necessary that we think of ourselves differently and meditate on the ways of God's life and what God desires of us. The meditations of our hearts should be from the sweet waters of the Word of God. The fountain of our heart is sweet, and the bitter

---

[143] (Rom. 12:1; Mt. 17:2)
[144] (Col. 3:10)
[145] (Tt. 3:5; Eph. 4:23)
[146] (Isa. 40:31; Eph. 4:24)
[147] (2 Cor. 4:16)

waters of the world must not be allowed to mix with it. Our minds that are inscribed with the Word of God must be consecrated to the governorship of the Holy Spirit and the rulership of the Word. We must not think like the world thinks, but give ourselves to thinking as God thinks. Through the mind of the Spirit that we now have, we have stepped into a whole new realm of possibilities in God. We can see what eyes have never seen before and hear what ears have never heard. It is our privilege to understand what has never entered into the heart of man. We are empowered to be conformed to the image of the Son and not to the world. Therefore, be renewed by thinking differently about yourselves in the light of Christ in you – this is a transfiguration that transcends every earthly care and human ability[148].

God demands purity of mind and purity of body, He gave it to us, and we must be willing to keep it. We could have never erased the iniquity of our past. We could have never been rid of a mind trained wrongly or a body given to unholy deeds. God in His mercy came and broke the bonds of sin so that we might begin anew. There is a new learning process: instead of being trained after this world, we are being trained in the mind of Christ and the ways of God's life. In the amazing mercy of God, we have been translated into this wonderful and mysterious realm of the Holy Spirit. The Teacher is continually moving us and

---

[148] (Eph. 4:23; Rom. 8:29; 12:1)

calling us to learn the ways of the life of the Spirit. The Holy Spirit pleads with us and pulls on us to come follow Him. The Word of God is visible before our eyes and made understandable in every human tongue. The presence of the Lord and His goodness surround us with the glory of His ways. The light is contrasted against the darkness; the good against the evil. It is up to each individual to choose if they will walk with God. Will you follow the Holy Spirit into this divine and unending life? Will you respond to His inspirations and strong convictions? He alone knows the way of life and the narrow path thereof – will you come follow Him? The voices and intercessions of Hell scream out along this narrow way, demanding that we hearken to their lust. You must be girded up in the spirit of your mind to give no thought to them. The Word of God and His presence are your sword and shield.

God desires that we think differently about ourselves – will we obey? If we continue to think of ourselves as anything less than co-inheritors with Christ, then we are not thinking according to God's plan. God has given us the spiritual weapons that we need to discern His will and bring into captivity every thought to the obedience of Christ[149]. We must recognize that Satan continues to go about with his lies and slander against the truth. We must refuse to hear the misleading ideas of men and the voice

---

[149] (2 Cor. 10:4)

of demon spirits. If we will believe the report of the Lord and hold fast to the confession of our faith, then we will see every miracle of God supplied to us as a result of our obedience to His Word. By the power of the new man, the former behavior and lust may be laid aside so that we can walk in God's image. We must be willing to take hold of the image of God and be renewed by the knowledge of that image[150]. To continue to view ourselves as weak, carnal, and unable to please God is the wrong way to think – there certainly is no renewed mind in that kind of thinking. Thinking after such a manner is giving place to the Devil and allowing sin to have dominion[151]. We are to move in faith and say as Mary did, "Be it unto me according to Your word." If we are unwilling to obey God and think of ourselves as a new creation who is called to the fullness of the maturity of Christ, then surely we will never realize such maturity, and we will find ourselves being tricked and misled by deceivers[152]. God's will and plan is that we be conformed to the image of His Son[153].

Come now, let your thoughts be bathed in the goodness and mercies of God. Be saturated with the ministry of the Holy Spirit and the mind of Christ. Let the utterances of God pour out of your heart and mind like the flowing rivers of paradise that produced every good

---

[150] (Col. 3:10)
[151] (Rom. 6:14; Eph. 4:27)
[152] (Eph. 4:14)
[153] (Rom. 8:29)

fruit. You have been made a partaker of His divine nature. You have escaped the corruption that is in the world through lust[154]. Now give yourself to a new kind of pleasure that only comes from above. God, who dwells within you, and the Spirit of the Son, who you possess, will show you how to walk in every strong desire and passion of the Holy One!

---

[154] (2 Pet. 1:4)

Forsake the Thoughts of Men

Regardless of who you are, God calls out to everyone, saying,

"Let the wicked forsake his way, and the unrighteous man his thoughts – and let him return unto the Lord, and He will have mercy upon him and will abundantly pardon."   *(Isaiah 55:7)*

The chief theme of the Gospel is repentance. God has made a way where there was no way. He has granted repentance unto life for all who will receive[155]. There is no reason to be controlled by evil and destroyed by sin. Your thoughts do not have to be dominated and ruined by the harassing and tormenting influences of demon spirits and wicked men. The immorality and gross violations against your soul and all humanity can be broken off right now. You can begin to enjoy the sweet communion of the Holy

---

[155] (Lk. 24:47; Ac. 11:18)

Spirit and the pleasantness of His life.

There are those who want God to receive them without any change of heart that results in a change of thinking or lifestyle. They have been deceived to believe that they can have a relationship with Jesus and continue on with their wickedness. However, this is far from being true — as far away as darkness is from light. Unfortunately, those who would believe and even teach such things have never tasted the pleasures and the goodness of this life of God. God cries out to us even as He did to ancient Israel saying, "...return every man from his evil way that I may forgive their iniquities and their sin"[156]. God has not changed His mind, but demands it all the more in this New Covenant. The ways of wickedness and sin will never be accepted by a holy God. He has provided a way to be made new, not a way to remain the same and yet be forgiven! The wages of sin is death, and the gift of eternal life is now available through Jesus Christ the Lord. You must be willing to accept this new and abundant life and forsake your wicked ways. The unholy thoughts of lust and iniquity must not be allowed. If you are willing, God will fill you with His own life and divine power. If you will forsake wickedness and sin, God will have mercy and abundantly pardon.

Being born again and made a new creation does not eliminate the influences of the demonic realm and past experiences. We will have to deal with the harassment and

---

[156] (Jer. 36:3)

accusations of Satan, the slanderer, but God has given us His divine power to demolish his works. As we give ourselves to the Holy Spirit and meditate upon God's Word, we grow in knowledge and spiritual understanding. We learn to let the peace of God rule our hearts and minds. Every unholy thought that belongs to fear and torment must be identified for what it is and not given dominion to displace the peace of God. Christ Jesus is the Prince of Peace who has given to us His peace so that we might be ruled and governed by peace. Strongholds of the mind and oppressing demon spirits that would attempt to impose their unholy thoughts must be identified for what they are and not allowed. We may have to fight a battle in our minds, but God has given us His power to win every time. We must be able to discern between our thoughts, as the redeemed, and the thoughts that come from the realms of the demonic. Understanding that our thoughts spring from the life of the Holy Spirit within gives us clear discernment about those thoughts that are the assailing powers of darkness at work against us. If we are deceived to believe that the desires of Satan are somehow our own desires, we lose before the battle begins. The battle line cannot be drawn with any greater contrast than the distinction of good and evil; what is of God and what is of Satan. We need a clear contrast defined for us between the peace that comes from the Prince of Peace and those things that belong to the world. The battle line is drawn, all that is in the world: the lust of the flesh, the lust of the eye, and the pride of life come from without and war against the love of the Father that dwells within[157].

Understanding the difference between the mind that belongs to the redeemed and the mind of the unregenerate state makes all the difference in winning the battle of the mind and forsaking the thoughts contrary to the mind of Christ. If we are uncertain of the source of our thoughts, a clear line of discernment can never be established. The wellspring of our heart brings forth the mind of Christ, because our hearts are the dwelling place of the Holy Spirit. Sin and iniquity, as well as doubt and unbelief, have no place in them. Once we have touched the realm of this heavenly communion in the Holy Spirit, there is a clear distinction made in our lives. God has caused us to know the truth, and we know that no lie is of the truth. The truth is found only in Christ Jesus and the Holy Spirit, who is the Spirit of truth.

One of the attributes of the mind is the ability to perceive things, both the natural and the spiritual. If the mind of man is to perceive the things of God, then it takes a miracle that only God can provide. God has given us that miracle so that we may know what is of the Spirit of God. The first occurrence in the New Testament of the Greek word for mind is found in Luke 24:45. It is there that we learn what only God can do for our minds. Christ

---

157 (1 Jn. 2:14-17)

Jesus opened up their minds (νοῦς, 'nous') so that they could understand the Scriptures. (Can there be anything that speaks more strongly to what it means to have a renewed mind and our thoughts enlightened by the grace of God?) Whereas Satan blinds the mind from understanding the works of God and His ways, the Holy Spirit enlightens us[158]. The Word of God enlightens our mind and causes us to know what pleases the Lord[159]. The mind can also be thought of as the "eyes of our understanding"[160]. The enlightenment of the "eyes of our understanding" allows us to see who God is and what He has done for us. This phrase may also be understood as "the eyes of our mind" from a linguistics perspective. The Greek word used in this verse is διάνοια ('dianoia'), which is related to νοῦς ('nous'). This word διάνοια ('dianoia'), like νοῦς ('nous'), may be translated as "mind" (LTW). The meaning can be more specifically understood as the way that the mind is directed (TDNT). God has given to us a new mind just as He has given to us a new heart. He has removed the blindness of mind and given us a mind that knows God and is submitted to God. We have the divine ability to discern what is of God and what is of the world. Discerning between the truth of God that is in our hearts and the lies and deceptions of Satan is part of the divine ability that God has given us. The mind is the

---

[158] (2 Cor. 4:3)
[159] (Ps. 19:18; 13:3)
[160] (Eph. 1:18)

faculty of man where things are understood and then communicated from. What's most important of all is that we can now love and serve God with all of our heart, soul, and mind (διάνοια, 'dianoia')[161].

---

[161] (Mt. 22:37)

The Great Confusion

So many have been confused by the teachings surrounding Romans 7, Galatians 5:17, and 1 Timothy 1:15. It has left them believing that after they have been redeemed and born again, they are still somehow under the dominion of sin, and they in turn refer to themselves as wretched sinners. This opinion does not agree with all of the other things that the Apostle Paul said about redemption and the new creation. It is essential that we understand Scripture in the context of all other Scripture, so we will take this last chapter of this book and show how Paul never viewed himself as a wretched man, or someone who was bound to the flesh-nature, or ever considered Himself as a sinner in Christ! Keep in mind that Romans 7 is set between Romans 6 and 8, which declare the true life of the born again saint. Romans 7 is the opposite message, concerning the life of the one living without this born again experience. Also, Galatians 5:17 is squarely placed between two verses of Scripture that, in agreement with the message of Christ Jesus, reinforce that we are born of the Spirit and thus we are empowered to live by the Spirit.

Romans 7 does not describe the life of Paul as a born-again believer. To think so is a violation of the context of the chapter as well as a violation of how he described himself after he was born again. Paul wrote in a representative style in Romans 7, describing the bondage of being under the Law and the sure futility of believing that one could be made righteous by the Law. Paul described the person that is under the Law as one who is carnal and not spiritual; under condemnation instead of living in the glorious liberty; bound to sin instead of free from sin. The person described in Romans 7 had no good thing in themselves, in great contrast to Christ Jesus reigning in a new creation. Very clearly, he was describing a person who "served the Law with their mind." The Apostle Paul was none of the things described in Romans 7:7-25.

Romans 7 opens up with the allegory of being dead to the Law and alive to Christ Jesus. The remainder of the chapter is about a person who is under the Law and serves the Law. Paul, in keeping with the things he repeatedly said elsewhere, makes it clear that those who are redeemed are no longer in the flesh (nature of sin) and that the motions of sins are no longer at work in their lives:

"For when <u>we were in the flesh</u>, the motions of sins, which were by the Law, worked in our members to bring forth fruit unto death. But now we are delivered from the Law, being dead to that which held us, so that we should serve in the newness of spirit and not in oldness of letter." (Romans 7:5–6)

Paul makes similar statements to this elsewhere, ensuring us that the "life of the flesh" refers to a life before being born of the Spirit. Romans 7 is about a person who is under the Law, serving the Law and bound by the flesh (the sin-nature). Paul had already made it clear that sin had no dominion over him or those who were born again[162]. He said that we are dead to sin and that the body of sin has been abolished[163]. The life that the believer is empowered to live is one that brings forth fruits unto holiness, not death as in Romans 7[164]. The old is gone, and the new has come. The new kind of life is the life of Christ Jesus[165]. He repeats over and over again that sin has no dominion over us[166]. In the chapter that follows, Paul made it very clear that <u>he is not in the flesh</u> but in the Spirit[167]. These statements alone are in direct contradiction to the unredeemed person that Paul

---

[162] (Rom. 6:1-23)
[163] (Rom. 6:2, 6)
[164] (Rom. 6:18)
[165] (Rom. 6:5)
[166] (Rom. 6:7, 12, 14, 22)
[167] (Rom. 8:9)

described in Romans 7. Sin was very much alive in the person under the Law that he was describing[168]. Sin had dominion and worked in the life of the person under the Law[169].

Paul did not serve the Law – He served God as a new creation. The person described in Romans 7 served the Law with their mind. Paul served God with His spirit, heart, and mind. He never confessed anywhere that He served sin with his flesh, but instead he confessed just the opposite. He made it clear many times that the body of the sins of the flesh had been removed, destroyed, and crucified[170]. Paul never repeated any of these things found in chapter 7, nor applied them to himself, anywhere in his Epistles.

Who was Paul? He was a man free set from sin and delivered from the Law by the blood of Jesus. The contradictions continue, because when he was under the Law and serving the Law, he described himself as blameless concerning the righteousness of the Law[171] – not guilty and condemned by the Law such as in Romans 7. And after he was delivered from the Law, he was a holy one, full of the Spirit, in whom Christ was dwelling[172]. He said concerning himself,

---

[168] (verses 9, 13, 20-21, 23, 25)
[169] (verses 11, 14, 15-19)
[170] (Col 2:11; Rom 6:6; Eph 4:22; Gal 2:22; Gal 5:24 etc)
[171] (Php. 3:6)
[172] (1 Thess. 1:5; Gal 2:20)

"You are witnesses, and God, how devoted and upright and blameless we were to you who believe."

(1 Thessalonians 2:10)

He was spiritual – not in the flesh, but in the Spirit[173]. He lived in a relationship with God where there was no condemnation, and he was a person who walked not after the flesh, but after the Spirit[174]. He was not led by the Law of commandments, but he was led by the Holy Spirit. Christ Jesus dwelled in Him. He was the temple of the Holy Spirit. Jesus Christ was manifested in his mortal body. He walked in the fullness of the blessing of the Gospel and fully preached the Gospel. Christ Jesus, the Son of God, was revealed in his life. The Word of God and the Spirit of God worked mightily within him[175]. All of these things concerning Paul are absolutely the opposite of those described about the person of Romans 7.

There are those that would suggest that 2 Corinthians 7:1 was proof that Paul believed that he was still in the flesh-nature. However, that is not at all what is represented by the need to "purify ourselves from every defilement of the flesh and spirit." To suggest such a thing takes the argument beyond the flesh-nature and denies that we have received a new spirit when we were born again. Paul

---

[173] (Rom. 8:9; 2 Tim 1:14)
[174] (Rom. 8:1, 9; 2 Cor. 3:9; 1 Cor. 2:4-17)
[175] (Rom. 15:19, 29; Ac. 19:10-11)

believed that our spirits are united with the Holy Spirit[176]. Surely with a new spirit, created by the new birth, our spirits now united with the Holy Spirit would be considered pure and untainted by the sins of the past. The intent of 2 Corinthians 7:1 is to emphasize that we are to mature in the holiness that we have received as a free gift.

To mature in holiness, we refuse the sin and iniquity of this world that would defile us. Christ Jesus is our righteousness and holiness, and we are in Him[177]. He is also in us and matures us in the righteousness and holiness that we have received from Him through the miracle of salvation[178]. We must put to death any sin or iniquity that would attempt to work in our bodies and defile the purity that has been given to us in Christ Jesus[179]. Our bodies and our spirits belong to God not to sin and iniquity[180]. We are commissioned not to allow the temple of the Lord to be defiled[181].

Understanding that the Greek word καθαρίσωμεν ('katharisomen') of 2 Corinthians 7:1 implies the same meaning as the Greek word θανατοῦτε ('thanatoute'), which is found in Romans 8:13. Whereas 'katharisomen' means "to purify," 'thanatoute' means "to put to death." As we mature in the holiness that we have received, we will be

---

[176] (1 Cor. 6:17)
[177] (1 Cor. 1:31)
[178] (Eph 4:13,15; Col 1:28)
[179] (Rom 8:13; Col 3:5)
[180] (1 Cor. 6:20; 1 Cor 3:16; 6:19; 2 Cor 6:16)
[181] (1 Cor 3:17)

attacked with every defilement of sin that the Tempter can throw at us. When defilers of our flesh or spirit come at us, we must "purify ourselves" of it, which is another way of saying that we must "put it to death." It is a radical way of expressing that we are not to allow any deeds of sin to work in our bodies. As Paul said previously, we are not to touch the "unclean thing"[182]. We are not to allow ourselves to be defiled by sin! Finally, the word for "flesh," σαρκὸς, ('sarkos'), which is used in 2 Corinthians 7:1, can be understood as a synonym for "body" (σώματος, 'somatos'), which is used in Romans 8:13. Finally, there is no proof that Paul meant to imply that the usage of "flesh" referred to the sin nature in 2 Corinthians 7:1.

Both in Romans 8:1-10 and in Galatians 5:16-23, Paul describes two different spiritual states of existence. He is not describing two spiritual conditions within a person, but two separate spiritual states! He describes the one, who is in an unregenerate state of the flesh, and the other, who was born of the Spirit and washed with the waters of regeneration. It is most certainly a reflection on the two separate states of existence that Jesus described in John 3:3-6 – the one who is born of the flesh and the one who is born of the Spirit. The most important point is that Paul says,

"If we walk in the Spirit, we will not fulfill the lust of

---

182 (2 Cor. 6:17)

the flesh."   *(Galatians 5:16)*

Why? Because the flesh (the demonic control over our lives) has been crucified, and we now find ourselves in Christ (the life of the Spirit).

"And they who are Christ's have crucified the flesh with the affections and lusts. If we live in the Spirit, let us also walk in the Spirit."   *(Galatians 5:24–25)*

The deeds of the flesh are manifested: adultery, fornication, lasciviousness, uncleanness, etc... These are the deeds of those who have no inheritance in the Kingdom of God[183]. It is the deeds of the unregenerate man bound in sin and death. These are basically the same deeds that were described by Jesus coming from the heart of the unredeemed: adultery, fornication, murder etc[184]. Just as Paul describes the two different states of being – those in the flesh compared to those in the Spirit in Romans 8:1-10 – he uses the same example in Galatians 5:17, 19-23. Everything about the Holy Spirit is opposite to the fallen and unredeemed nature of man. As opposite as God is from Satan, so the Holy Spirit is opposite from the nature of sin (the flesh). These two natures are distinct, separate, and opposite from one another and will never

---

[183] (Gal. 5:20)
[184] (Mk. 7:21)

agree. To conclude that these two natures, which are two separate states of existence, dwell in the believer is contrary to the message of the new creation. It is contrary to the context that emphatically states that we are in the Spirit and not in the flesh[185].

If a person is in bondage to sin, they cannot do what they want to do, just as Paul described in Romans 7:14-17. The redeemed, having been given the life of the Holy Spirit, are not to do their own will but are to follow the leadership of the Holy Spirit. When a person is in the "flesh", the unredeemed state, they cannot do what they please[186]. Also, when a person is in the Spirit, they are to be submitted to the will of the Holy Spirit and not walk after their own self-interest but instead are to do what the Father desires[187]. For example: if we are led by the Holy Spirit, we are going to walk in the love that He supplies to us. The works of the flesh, on the other hand, which are adultery, fornication, etc are opposite of divine love. When a person is bound to the sin-nature, they obey the strong impulses of sin. Now that we have the Spirit of life within us, we can say "no" to all that is in the world: the lust of the flesh, the lust of the eye, and the pride of life. We are empowered to love like God loves by the Holy Spirit and say no to the abusive powers of lust. We now are to walk after the laws of life and do the will of the Father, not our

---

[185] (Gal. 5:16, 18, 24-25; Rom 8:9)
[186] (Rom. 7:14-17)
[187] (Rom. 8:5; Jn. 15:5)

own[188]. We do not walk after the flesh, but after the Spirit, because we have now been born of the Spirit[189].

Jesus said,

"That which is born of the flesh is flesh, and that which is born of the Spirit is spirit." (John 3:6)

These are two separate states of existence. Paul concludes with a similar statement regarding those who are born-again in Romans 8 when he said, "But you are not in the flesh but in the Spirit..."[190] – once again, these are two separate states of existence. As long as the Law ruled, the life of God was not imparted, and the fallen nature, which Paul referred to the old man, reigned in the heart of man[191]. But now for the redeemed, the old is gone and the new has come, and the life that we live is one in the Spirit[192]. Paul made it very clear that we are free from the law of sin and death, the old man, and his nature[193]. The righteousness of the Law is fulfilled in us, because we do not walk in the flesh (the old man and his corrupt nature), but we walk according to the Spirit[194]. Those who are of the flesh mind the things of the flesh, but we belong to the

---

[188] (Rom. 8:2)
[189] (Rom. 8:1)
[190] (Rom. 8:9)
[191] (Gal. 3:21; Rom. 6:4)
[192] (Gal. 5:16, 18; Jn. 3:6; 2 Cor. 5:17; Tt. 3:5 etc)
[193] (Rom. 8:2; 6:4; Col. 2:11)
[194] (Rom. 8:4; 3:21)

Spirit, having been born of the Spirit, and we mind the things of the Spirit[195]. One is ruled by death; the other is ruled by life and peace[196]. One is the enemy of God and opposed to everything about Him; the other is one with Him[197]. Finally, there is no one in the spiritual state of the flesh that can please God[198].

Did Paul believe that He was a sinner? No! Paul said,

"But if, while we seek to be made righteous in Christ, we are also found to be sinners, is Christ then the minister of sin? It cannot be!" (Galatians 2:17)

Throughout Paul's Epistles, he identifies himself in an opposite way from the description that is given in Romans 7. He made it clear that we are not to continue in sin[199]. He referred to himself, and all believers, as being in Christ Jesus and as being righteous and holy. There is only one place that it can even be suggested that he thought of himself as a sinner after he was born again, and that is 1 Timothy 1:15. However, we can understand 1 Timothy 1:15 in more than one way. If we conclude that he believed himself to be a sinner, it is not witnessed anywhere else in his Epistles and is contrary to what he said about himself

---

[195] (Rom. 8:5; Jn. 3:6; Tt. 3:5)
[196] (Rom. 8:6)
[197] (Rom. 8:7; 1 Cor 2:14; Jn 14:17)
[198] (Rom. 8:8)
[199] (Rom. 6:1, 15)

many times. Therefore, without a second witness, and with contradictory evidence, we must look to understand what He said in view of all the other witnesses that he gave of himself.

What was Paul referring to when he said, "Christ Jesus came into the world to save sinners, of whom I am first"?[200] How are we to understand this phrase, "of whom I am first" (ὧν πρῶτός εἰμι ἐγώ)? First of all, this phrase may be understood as a historical present tense. This is the use of a present tense to describe something that happened in the past (D. Wallace 1996). Paul viewed himself as first in rank (πρῶτός, 'protos') as a sinner because of those things that he did ignorantly before he met Jesus, as He described in the previous verse,

"Who was before a blasphemer, and a persecutor, and violent, but I was shown mercy because ignorant, I did it in unbelief."   *(1 Timothy 1:13)*

What must be appreciated is that Paul never described any acts of sin in his life after salvation, but rather just the opposite. He referred to himself as blameless in his behavior and demanded it from everyone who would be a leader in the church[201]. There is not one verse in all of the Epistles of Paul where he describes himself to be anything

---

[200] (1 Tim. 1:15)
[201] (Php. 2:15; 1 Thess. 5:23; 1 Tim. 3:2, 10; Tt. 1:7; 2;12)

other than walking in the Spirit and revealing the life of Christ Jesus. In fact, he made it very clear how a person that was called a brother was to be treated if they had ongoing sin — they were to be shunned and even openly rebuked[202].

---

[202] (1 Cor. 5:11-13; 1 Tim. 5:20; 2 Thess. 3:6, 14-15; Tt. 3:10; Rom. 16:17)

Conclusion

We have been redeemed by the blood of Jesus and recreated in the likeness of God by the Holy Spirit through the new birth. We are not supposed to give any place to the Devil in our lives – which includes any power over us or opportunity to lead us astray[203]. We are going to be tempted by the Tempter. We are going to have to deal with all of the lust and sin of this world but God has given us dominion through Jesus Christ our Sovereign Ruler. It is a fatal error to give Satan and any form of sin a place of dominion over our lives. We must recognize that Satan was completely defeated at the cross. He was stripped of all his power over the person who puts their trust in Christ Jesus and is born-again[204]. Jesus destroyed Satan through His death and brought resurrection power to those who will believe[205]. He gave us complete dominion over all the works of the Devil so we could tread upon

---

[203] (Eph. 4:27; Jam. 4:7; 1 Pet. 5:9)
[204] (Col. 2:15)
[205] (Heb. 2:14)

them, and there would be no way that they could touch or harm us[206]. Paul said that Jesus abolished death and brought life and immortality to light through the Gospel[207]. Jesus said that the prince of this world (Satan) is cast out – referring to the complete loss of Satan's power over the ones who put their trust in Jesus[208]. Jesus is King and exalted far above all things. There is no power that can usurp His rulership and we are in His kingdom!

If we will stand in the liberty that has been given to us in Jesus, there is no power that can take us into bondage against our will[209]. It is essential however, that we do not allow the satanic realm to convince us that they have any power over our lives. The entirety of the message of this book is to convince those who are born again that they are seated together with Christ Jesus far above the powers of darkness/ We must not believe for a second that we are powerless against the devices of our enemy or powerless to say no to sin. Jesus was manifested to destroy the works of the Devil and has given us the blessing of living in His conquest[210]. Our authority over all the powers of darkness is certain. We have been commissioned to cast out demons with the authority of Jesus Christ. We have been empowered to set humanity free from every influence of

---

[206] (Lk. 10:19; 1 Jn. 5:18; Mk. 16:17; Mt. 10:1)
[207] (2 Tim. 1:10; Rom. 8:2)
[208] (Jn. 12:31)
[209] (Gal. 5:1; Jn. 8:32, 36; Rom. 6:18; 8:2; 2 Cor. 3:17)
[210] (1 Jn. 3:8)

sin and death. We have been given the authority to turn men from darkness to light and to deliver them from the power of Satan to God[211].

We have been made one with God and commissioned to stand in Christ Jesus' stead[212]. God has empowered us with His power from on High to do the works of Jesus and greater works. We have the strength of the Lord and the power of His might[213]. He has made us more than conquerors and given to us the overcoming power to defeat Satan at every point[214]. However, if we do not believe what God has said, then we will never walk in the miracle of salvation that has made us, and fashioned us after the inward likeness of God. We will never realize that the greater One is on the inside of us and that He is far greater than "he who is in the world." If we are to believe for a moment that the power of Satan reigns from within, and that we must obey his desires, we have not believed the report of the Lord. God said that He dwells within us[215]. The fundamental cardinal doctrine of the New Testament is- Christ Jesus dwells within our lives[216]. Jesus said that if the Son shall set you free (from sin) then you shall absolutely be free[217]. We are the temples of the Holy

---

[211] (Ac. 26:18)
[212] (Jn. 6:56; 14:21-23; 17:21-22)
[213] (Eph. 6:10)
[214] (2 Cor. 2:14; 1 Jn. 2:14; 4:4; 5:4-5; Rom. 8:37)
[215] (Jn. 14:17-23; 2 Cor. 6:16-18; 1 Jn. 3:24 etc)
[216] (Col. 1:27; Jn. 6:56; 2 Cor. 5:17 etc)
[217] (Jn. 8:34-36)

Spirit[218]. We must not listen to the lies and propaganda of the enemy that would try to convince us that we are still under their power and dominion. Satan would lie and say that we are not really free, but who are we going to believe? If we believe a lie, we will be defeated before we ever engage in the war. The truth of God's Word makes known that Satan has been totally defeated by Jesus. Now we are also empowered with God's own power to defeat every demonic influence that we have to face. The faith that we have received overcomes the world and the prince and the power of the world[219]. All we must do is submit ourselves to God and resist the Devil steadfast in the faith and he will flee!

---

[218] (1 Cor. 3:16; 6:19; 2 Cor. 6:16)
[219] (1 Jn 2:13; 4:4; 5:4-5)

References

Campbell C., (2012) Paul and Union with Christ

King James Version, Electronic Edition of the 1900 Authorized Version.

LTD – Douglas Mangum, Derek R. Brown, et al., eds., Lexham Theological Wordbook, Lexham Bible Reference Series (Bellingham, WA: Lexham Press, 2014).

The New Testament in the original Greek: Byzantine textform / compiled and arranged by Maurice A. Robinson and William G. Pierpont. (2005)

TDNT – Gerhard Kittel, Geoffrey W. Bromiley, and Gerhard Friedrich, eds., Theological Dictionary of the New Testament (Grand Rapids, MI: Eerdmans, 1964–).

Translation in the Oldest Tradition, Dr. Mark Spitsbergen (2020)

Wallace D. Greek (1996) Grammar Beyond the Basics: An Exegetical Syntax of the New Testament.

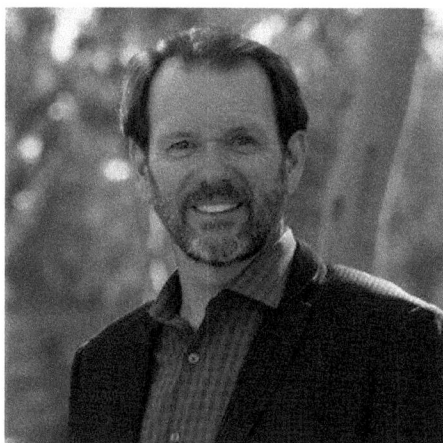

About the Author

Dr. Mark Spitsbergen is the Senior Pastor of the Abiding Place in San Diego, California where he and his wife Anne have pastored since 1985. He holds a Bachelor of Arts Degree (BA) in Biology/Chemistry from Point Loma Nazarene University, a Master of Science (MS) from the University of Saint Andrews, a Doctorate of Theology (ThD) from School of Bible Theology, as well as a Doctorate of Ministry (D. Min.) from Life Christian University. He has been studying Biblical languages since 1983. He began his study of biblical languages at PLNU and also studied at UCSD with Dr. David Noel Freedman.

www.ingramcontent.com/pod-product-compliance
Lightning Source LLC
Chambersburg PA
CBHW072359090426
42741CB00012B/3089